AMPLIFY
YOUR IMPACT

COACHING COLLABORATIVE
TEAMS IN PLCS AT WORK®

foreword by **REBECCA DUFOUR**

THOMAS W.
MANY

MICHAEL J.
MAFFONI

SUSAN K.
SPARKS

TESHA FERRIBY
THOMAS

Solution Tree | Press

a division of
Solution Tree

555 North Morton Street
Bloomington, IN 47404
800.733.6786 (toll free) / 812.336.7700
FAX: 812.336.7790

email: info@SolutionTree.com
SolutionTree.com

Visit **go.SolutionTree.com/PLCbooks** to download the free reproducibles in this book.

Printed in the United States of America

22   21   20   19   18   5

Library of Congress Cataloging-in-Publication Data

Names: Many, Thomas W., author.
Title: Amplify your impact : coaching collaborative teams in PLCs at work /
    Thomas W. Many, Michael J. Maffoni, Susan K. Sparks, and Tesha Ferriby
    Thomas.
Description: Bloomington, IN : Solution Tree Press, [2018] | Includes
    bibliographical references and index.
Identifiers: LCCN 2017041910 | ISBN 9781945349324 (perfect bound)
Subjects: LCSH: Teachers--In-service training--United States. | Professional
    learning communities--United States. | Teachers--Professional
    relationships--United States. | School improvement programs--United States.
Classification: LCC LB1731 .M336 2018 | DDC 370.71/10973--dc23 LC record available at https://
lccn.loc.gov/2017041910

Solution Tree
Jeffrey C. Jones, CEO
Edmund M. Ackerman, President

Solution Tree Press
President and Publisher: Douglas M. Rife
Editorial Director: Sarah Payne-Mills
Art Director: Rian Anderson
Managing Production Editor: Caroline Cascio
Senior Production Editor: Suzanne Kraszewski
Senior Editor: Amy Rubenstein
Copy Editor: Ashante K. Thomas
Proofreader: Evie Madsen
Text and Cover Designer: Abigail Bowen
Editorial Assistants: Jessi Finn and Kendra Slayton

To Jane, who showed us the impact coaching can have on collaborative teams, and to the grandkids—Mary, Maggie, and Leo—who inspire us to continue the work of improving schools.

—TOM MANY

To Caroline, I am blessed to love, dream, and walk hand in hand with you through life. Your belief in me is humbling. To Luca, my "bringer of light," you're a true gift that embodies all that is good. To Grace, you made me whole and fill me with sparkles, sunshine, and hope. My heart is home.

To Mom and Dad, you engrained in me the importance of love and family while encouraging me to push my own limits and make a difference. You love unconditionally and lead by example. The shadow you cast is wonderful and vast, and I am forever comfortable living within it.

My sincere appreciation goes to Jefferson County Public Schools and the PLC team for continuing to believe.

Finally, my heartfelt gratitude to Tom Many for bringing me along on this joyous ride. I have received far more than I have offered and continue to learn from our partnership. I am forever in debt to you.

—MICHAEL MAFFONI

To parents who have the opportunity to be the most influential educators of all. And to mine, Jim and Jan Sparks, who took that responsibility to heart. I love you.

—SUSAN SPARKS

This book is dedicated to Tony for showing me the meaning of true love, to Bob and Theresa for teaching me the value of education, to Jennifer for supporting me no matter what the situation, and to Elise for being a constant source of pride and joy. Thank you for shaping me into the person I am today, and for your unconditional love and support.

I would also like to express my sincere gratitude to Ryan McLeod, Paul Szymanski, and the hundreds of dedicated staff members at the East Detroit Public Schools. Your commitment to high levels of learning for all students makes a difference for kids every single day. To my colleagues and friends at the Macomb Intermediate School District, I thank you for your ongoing encouragement and for the endless support you give the educators and children in Macomb County on a daily basis. Finally, heartfelt thanks go to my coauthor and mentor, Thomas Many, without whom this book would never have been possible.

—TESHA THOMAS

ACKNOWLEDGMENTS

We would like to acknowledge those who helped us frame the idea for this book. We hope it will spark a conversation about the importance of coaching collaborative teams around improving their professional learning community practices.

We are also grateful to Becky DuFour for her support and inspiration; to the entire team at Solution Tree Press for their extraordinary professionalism; to Douglas Rife for being so accessible and encouraging; and to Suzanne Kraszewski for her incredible patience, guidance, and expertise. We could not have completed this project without important contributions from each and every one of you!

Finally, we appreciate the comments and suggestions of Brenda Kaylor, Chris Bryan, Cindy Harrison, and many other coaching advocates from across the United States. We are especially thankful for the contributions of our colleagues in the East Detroit Public Schools and Jefferson County Public Schools.

Solution Tree Press would like to thank the following reviewers:

Emily Anderson
Instructional Coach
Marlin Elementary School
Bloomington, Indiana

Stephanie Hodgins
Freshman Head Principal
Klein Oak High School
Klein, Texas

Janna Cochrane
Principal
North Greenville Elementary School
Greenville, Wisconsin

JR Kuch
Principal
Clinton High School
Clinton, Iowa

Renee Collins
Secondary Instructional Coach
Pleasantville Community
  School District
Pleasantville, Iowa

Kathy Liston
Instructional Coach
Brookview Elementary School
West Des Moines, Iowa

Josh McMahon
Principal
Morton West High School
Berwyn, Illinois

Debra Prenkert
Principal
Clear Creek Elementary School
Bloomington, Indiana

Joseph Powell
Science Instructional Coach
James Bowie High School
Austin, Texas

Visit **go.SolutionTree.com/PLCbooks** to download
the free reproducibles in this book.

TABLE OF CONTENTS

PART I

CHAPTER I

CHAPTER 2

Coaching Collaborative Teams in a PLC 27

PART II

CHAPTER 3

Amplifying Your Impact With Clarity 47

ABOUT THE AUTHORS

 **Thomas W. Many** is an educational consultant in Denver, Colorado. Tom retired as the superintendent of schools in Kildeer Countryside CCSD 96 in Buffalo Grove, Illinois. Tom's career included twenty years of experience as superintendent, in addition to serving as a classroom teacher, learning center director, curriculum supervisor, principal, and assistant superintendent. District 96 earned the reputation as a place where the faculty and administration worked together to become one of the premier elementary school districts in the United States during his tenure as superintendent.

Tom has worked with developing professional learning communities in school districts around the world. He has proven to be a valuable resource to those schools beginning their journey, offering special insights into developing a culture that supports the creation of high-performing collaborative teams.

In addition to more than fifty articles, Tom is the coauthor of *Learning by Doing: A Handbook for Professional Learning Communities at Work, Third Edition* with Richard DuFour, Rebecca DuFour, Robert Eaker, and Mike Mattos; coauthor of *Concise Answers to Frequently Asked Questions* with Mike Mattos, Richard DuFour, Rebecca DuFour, and Robert Eaker; a contributing author in *The Collaborative Teacher: Working Together as a Professional Learning Community*; coauthor of *Aligning School Districts as PLCs* with Mark Van Clay and Perry Soldwedel; and coauthor of *How to Cultivate Collaboration in a PLC* and *Leverage: Using PLCs to Promote Lasting Improvement in Schools* with Susan K. Sparks.

To learn more about Tom's work, follow @tmany96 on Twitter.

Michael J. Maffoni, an educator since 1987, has a diverse background that includes experience as a teacher, principal, and district administrator in a variety of districts and school settings in Colorado. He also teaches courses in educational leadership as an affiliate faculty member at Regis University.

Michael is the director of professional learning communities for Jefferson County Public Schools, Golden, Colorado. In this current role, Michael leads PLC implementation in over one hundred schools throughout the district. His collaborative leadership has been instrumental in developing an integrated PLC support system, monitoring structure, and associated professional learning for district leaders, principals, instructional coaches, and teachers.

Michael's professional passion focuses on increasing educator and student learning through creating agency to coach and support collaborative teams. He has presented at state and national events on topics related to a cycle of continuous improvement to support schools, teams, and individual educators. Michael has coauthored articles on increasing the effectiveness of collaborative teams.

Michael earned a master's degree in education/administration and supervision from the University of Phoenix and a bachelor's degree in education from the University of Wyoming.

To learn more about Michael's work, follow @mjmaffoni64 on Twitter.

Susan K. Sparks is an educational consultant in Denver, Colorado. Susan retired in 2008 as the executive director of the Front Range BOCES (board of cooperative educational services) for Teacher Leadership, a partnership with the University of Colorado at Denver. Susan spent her career in St. Vrain Valley School District as a teacher and with four different BOCES as staff developer, assistant director, and executive director. She consults internationally in collaborative cultures, conflict resolution, contract negotiations, and community engagement.

She provides professional development and training in facilitating professional learning communities, impacting results through interpersonal effectiveness, managing challenging conversations, and creating collaborative teams.

Susan contributed to *The Collaborative Teacher: Working Together as a Professional Learning Community* and coauthored *How to Cultivate Collaboration in a PLC* and *Leverage: Using PLCs to Promote Lasting Improvement in Schools.*

To learn more about Susan's work, follow @sparks12_susan on Twitter.

 **Tesha Ferriby Thomas** is a school improvement facilitator and language arts consultant at the Macomb Intermediate School District in Macomb County, Michigan. She has worked in this capacity since 2012, supporting struggling districts and school leaders by helping them embed systemic practices that result in improved student achievement. Her passion for the power of PLCs has grown over twenty years as she has worked to support PLC implementation as a teacher, department chairperson, assistant principal, and assistant superintendent for curriculum and instruction. She presents regularly at local, state, and national conferences on topics ranging from developing text-dependent questions to implementing an instructional learning cycle in a PLC. She has been a member of the Michigan Learning Forward board and the Michigan Department of Education Surveys of Enacted Curriculum Steering Committee, and is a National Writing Project fellow. She is also a doctoral candidate at the University of Michigan-Flint where she is researching the impact of coaching on PLCs.

To learn more about Tesha's work, follow @tferribythomas on Twitter.

To book Thomas W. Many, Michael J. Maffoni, Susan K. Sparks, or Tesha Ferriby Thomas for professional development, contact pd@SolutionTree.com.

FOREWORD

By Rebecca DuFour

In *Amplify Your Impact: Coaching Collaborative Teams in PLCs at Work®*, authors Thomas W. Many, Michael J. Maffoni, Susan K. Sparks, and Tesha Ferriby Thomas sound a clarion call for supporting the most valuable resources available to students: collaborative teams of teachers who take collective responsibility for the learning success of each student entrusted to them. The mission of Professional Learning Communities (PLCs) at Work schools and districts—ensuring high levels of learning for all—can only be realized through a collaborative culture in which educators work in teams that take collective responsibility for each student's learning. The authors of *Amplify Your Impact* contend that coaching collaborative teams by providing clarity, feedback, and support helps teams in PLC schools become high performing sooner, and, thus, teams help more students learn at higher levels sooner. I wholeheartedly agree!

Since the late-1990s, I have had the privilege of being both a student and teacher of the PLC at Work process. In my second tenure as an elementary principal, soon after I read *Professional Learning Communities at Work: Best Practices for Enhancing Student Achievement* (DuFour & Eaker, 1998), I was honored to work with a very dedicated staff that embraced and implemented the structural and cultural changes necessary to ensure high levels of learning for all. We *learned together* about the PLC process by reading, by attending workshops, and mostly by doing, failing, and trying again more intelligently. As we applied our new learning in the context of our own school, we soon recognized that the collaborative teams of teachers within our school were the engines driving continuous improvement. We also recognized that even though all of the teams in our school were focused on the same work—addressing the critical questions of learning—each team, comprised of members with different personalities and strengths, developed its own unique culture. We learned that different teams had different needs at different times. Teacher leaders and I responded as quickly as we could to each team's needs, but honestly, in our first year of engaging in the PLC process, we provided both *just-in-time* and *sorry-this-is-late* support as we did our best to help teams work at the right work.

Now, like the authors and experienced PLC practitioners of *Amplify Your Impact*, we have collectively witnessed that same experience in hundreds and thousands of schools. We have seen schools at every level—early childhood, elementary, middle, and high school—in countries across the globe in a variety of settings—urban, suburban, and rural—engage in this proven, ongoing process of continuous improvement. But unlike our work in the late-1990s, we have never had greater clarity on what it takes to improve schools and districts, regardless of their level or location.

- Educators work in collaborative teams and take collective responsibility for student learning.

- Collaborative teams implement a guaranteed and viable curriculum, unit by unit.

- Collaborative teams monitor student learning through an ongoing assessment process that includes frequent, team-developed common formative assessments.

- Collaborative teams use the results of common assessments to:

    - Intervene and extend learning on behalf of students

    - Improve individual practice

    - Build the team's capacity to achieve its goals

- The school provides a systematic process for intervention and extension, based on the results of each team's common assessments.

If collaborative teams are the fundamental building blocks of a PLC school (and they are), and if collaborative teams in PLC schools are going to focus on the right work (and they must), then the leadership team of the school must work to ensure collaborative teams have everything they'll need to be successful in the work they must do. As teams dig into each critical issue that impacts student learning, the coaches of collaborative teams must provide the clarity, feedback, support, encouragement, and appreciation necessary for teams to continue to learn and grow in the *right work*. To their great credit, the authors of *Amplify Your Impact* present specific and powerful research, protocols, tools, tips, and strategies on how schools and districts can ensure coaching for collaborative teams in the PLC at Work process.

If you recognize the need for significant structural and cultural shifts in our schools and want to learn at a deeper level about the work of collaborative teams and how coaching those teams can enhance and accelerate the teams' impact on student learning, then you absolutely have the right book in your hands. *Amplify Your Impact* will supply you with what you need to provide clarity, feedback, and support to the engines of continuous improvement.

INTRODUCTION

At some time in our lives, a coach has inspired most of us. It may have been a little league coach, a Girl Scouts leader, or even a family member who encouraged us and helped us focus on a personal goal we were trying to reach. We appreciated the coach's interest and felt special when he or she volunteered his or her time to help us improve. This coach cared about us and our success, which motivated us to try even harder. As professionals, we still need coaches in our corner spurring us on, reminding us of our strengths and helping us overcome our weaknesses.

Coaching is not a new idea in schools. In fact, 21st century coaching models that focus on improving the instructional practice of individual teachers are considered *best practice*. With this book, we seek to move from best practice to *next practice*—from coaching models focused on individual teachers to a coaching framework focused on collaborative teams. We consider this shift the next generation of best practice. We are already seeing schools and districts beginning to shift their coaching efforts from individuals to teams, and in doing so, they *amplify* the positive effects both coaching *and* collaboration have on teaching and learning.

Collaboration is not a new idea in schools either, and the Professional Learning Communities at Work® (PLC) process—"an ongoing process in which educators work collaboratively in recurring cycles of collective inquiry and action research to achieve better results for the students they serve" (DuFour, DuFour, Eaker, Many, & Mattos, 2016, p. 10)—creates learning environments in which learning is constant, and innovation and experimentation flourish.

Highly effective collaborative teams have been called the foundation, the fundamental building block, and the engine that drives a PLC (Eaker & Dillard, 2017). In many schools, principals have taken the first step and created time for teams to meet during the regular school day and then encouraged teams to "go forth and collaborate." Time is a necessary condition for collaboration, but time alone is not enough. If the goal is to build a collaborative culture, it will take more—a lot more—than a dedicated and protected time for teams to meet. Functioning as an effective member of a collaborative team likely will require new learning on the part of teachers. Team members must become skilled at things like how to create norms and SMART goals, how to use protocols with assessment data, and how to build trust and manage conflict, all while engaging in a process of collective inquiry that has an action orientation and using cycles of continuous improvement with a clear focus on results. As Robert Garmston and Bruce Wellman suggest (1999), "In many respects, collaboration needs to be taught." They continue, "The capacity to be a colleague is different from other capacities of good teaching" (p. 24).

As DuFour and his colleagues (2016) explain, becoming a PLC is a journey, not a destination. The PLC journey is a transformation because it constitutes a complete shift in how educators and school leaders do their everyday business. This book is about *coaching* the PLC process. It is intended to serve as a resource for those schools and districts that are beginning or are already on their journey to becoming a PLC and want to accelerate that transformation.

If the goal is to improve teaching and learning in our schools, and if the PLC process is the strategy school and district leaders choose to reach that goal, then leaders must help teacher teams improve their PLC practices. Robert Eaker and Heather Dillard (2017) suggest that, "Just as it is generally recognized that districts must work to close learning gaps between subgroups, it is also district leaders' responsibility to close the effectiveness gap between collaborative teams within each school" (p. 46). By combining the most effective aspects of coaching and collaboration, we believe teams can develop the knowledge and skills necessary to become fully functioning and highly successful within their larger PLC. This book serves as a guide for schools and districts that are committed to the development of highly effective collaborative teams.

A Coaching Framework

In order to coach collaborative teams in PLCs, we combine the latest research on coaching and collaboration to offer a coaching framework that improves the effectiveness of collaborative teams in diverse school settings. Three important concepts— (1) clarity, (2) feedback, and (3) support—are the cornerstones of the coaching framework we describe in this book.

Clarity

Before teachers can benefit from the power of collaboration, they must understand what it takes to fully implement the PLC model. As Mike Schmoker (2004) states, "Clarity precedes competence" (p. 10). Our experience shows that one of the differences between teams operating as either *PLC lite* or *PLC right* is a thorough understanding of the PLC process. An excellent way to build shared knowledge about PLCs is to involve teachers in creating a strategy implementation guide (SIG) that describes the specific behaviors we associate with successful PLCs. Engaging the faculty and staff in the process of developing a SIG promotes clarity, builds shared knowledge, creates ownership, and encourages the development of a common vocabulary. It also establishes a standard of best PLC practice and allows teams to measure their progress toward becoming high-performing collaborative teams. Clarity is the first cornerstone of a framework for coaching collaborative teams.

Feedback

The second cornerstone, feedback, is vital for teams to improve. As Grant Wiggins (2010) writes, feedback is "how learning occurs" (p. 1). This coaching framework takes great care to emphasize the importance of providing teams with frequent opportunities for effective feedback. Not all teams learn new skills at the same time or in the same ways, so when working with collaborative teams, coaches provide differentiated levels of feedback depending on each individual team's needs. Feedback anchored in an agreed-on standard and described in a SIG allows teams and coaches to hold data-driven conversations, chart next steps, and launch action plans.

Support

The third cornerstone of this coaching framework is support. Teams thrive when clarity and feedback become the basis for specific support. We argue that improved PLC practices require clarity around expectations, differentiated feedback anchored in an agreed-on standard of best practice, and specific strategies that support collaborative teams.

The coaching framework described in the remainder of this book is grounded in the cornerstone concepts of clarity, feedback, and support. Individually, each of these can contribute to a team's effectiveness, but when clarity is combined with the kind of effective feedback that identifies specific support a team needs to succeed, the productivity of collaborative teams is amplified.

Figure I.1 (page 4) shows the framework for coaching we explore in this book.

Becoming a high-functioning collaborative team is a process. However, the process is not linear, and the path looks different for each team. Like collaboration, the coaching process is recursive, and factors like team member composition, skill sets, content, and other outside influences may interrupt the cycle. Veterans of the PLC process know that diversions are normal and that leaders must proactively plan for them. However, getting teams that do take a wrong turn back on track and remaining focused can be a challenge. We advocate the intentional coaching of collaborative teams as a way to sustain the PLC process.

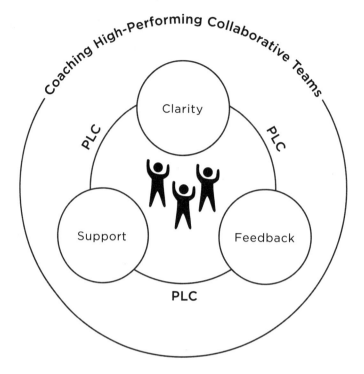

Figure I.1: A framework for coaching in a PLC.

Three Reasons

We believe this framework makes sense for three main reasons.

1. Coaching allows collaborative teams to develop a higher level of precision around their PLC practice.

2. The resources (context, content, and coaches) necessary to support the coaching of collaborative teams are well within the reach of every school.

3. Coaching provides collaborative teams within a PLC with the missing link between learning and doing.

Coaching Helps Develop Greater Precision With PLC Practice

We believe coached teams are more likely to implement the new practices they are learning (such as common assessments and schoolwide systems of intervention) more frequently and at a more accelerated rate than uncoached teams are. Clarity allows teams to be more precise in their understanding of the why, how, and what of the PLC process. For example, coached teams better understand why teachers collaborate, how teams use data, and what all students should know and be able to do.

Coached teams—those that regularly receive focused and effective feedback—have a more accurate understanding of where they are, where they need to be, and what they need to do to improve their practice. We believe that coached teams, more so than uncoached teams, are able to clearly articulate the purpose and appropriate use of the new practices they are learning (such as norms, protocols, and SMART goals).

Finally, coached teams benefit from support that is both specific and targeted. Because coaches are able to deploy a range of resources that provide the right people with the right kind of assistance at the right time, we believe that coached teams are more likely than uncoached teams to build the kind of capacity and requisite skills necessary to facilitate their own work.

Coaching Resources Are Available to Every School

According to Joellen Killion and Cindy Harison (2017), "Learning with one's teammates provides the context for effective learning for teachers" (p. 163); thus, the context for the coaching framework we envision is a collaborative team operating within the larger PLC.

The content coaches should focus on when working within this framework consists of those practices that are most closely aligned with the three big ideas and the four critical questions (DuFour et al., 2016) that are so fundamental to the PLC process.

We also believe that those who use this framework to coach collaborative teams should not be limited to individuals whose job descriptions include the word *coach*. Killion and Harrison (2017) define coaching as, "a process that engages one professional with another to clarify and achieve goals" (p. 6). For the purposes of this framework, we take a more inclusive view of coaching and consider a wide range of roles within PLCs as potential coaches for collaborative teams.

For us it's about *coaching* not *coaches*, and while not every school employs coaches, most schools likely have some combination of principals, assistant principals, department chairs, PLC leaders, district-level coordinators, curriculum specialists, or teacher leaders who can help teams improve their practice. We believe there are lots of people who can be involved in coaching others to higher levels of performance.

Coaching Provides the Missing Link Between Learning and Doing

We believe the conscious, purposeful, and intentional coaching of collaborative teams within a PLC has tremendous potential for improving schools. The framework we describe provides the missing link between learning and doing.

Principals often ask, "Why hasn't all the training translated into changes in our practice?" They wonder aloud, "What is preventing us from moving from theory into practice, from learning into doing?" The answer to these questions has been right in front of us all along: the very best way to move a school from PLC lite to PLC right is by coaching collaborative teams.

About This Book

Throughout the rest of this book, we present the framework specifics for coaching collaborative teams. We recognize that calling on schools to shift limited resources from coaching individual teachers to coaching collaborative teams will challenge current thinking and change existing practice. Our hope is that we cause school leaders to pause and consider the possibilities that such a shift would create.

This book is divided into three parts. Part I focuses on the *why*, *how*, and *what* of coaching collaborative teams. In chapter 1, we delve into the research around collaboration and coaching to build a rationale in support of a shift from coaching individual teachers to coaching collaborative teams. In chapter 2, we further describe the connection between the PLC model and a framework for coaching teams. The chapter concludes with a case study of two school systems to illustrate the impact that the successful execution of an integrated approach to coaching teams has on student learning.

Part II of the book explores the relationship between the cornerstone concepts of clarity, feedback, and support and provides a practical framework for coaching collaborative teams. In chapter 3, we share our tool for coaching collaborative teams, the SIG, and describe a practical process a school or district can use to develop its own SIG. When coaches regularly use a SIG, they help teams clarify expectations, identify current reality, and pinpoint next steps members will need to take to improve their PLC practice. In chapter 4, we explore the essential role feedback plays in improving a team's PLC practices. Effective feedback is essential to improvement. We define several types of feedback and offer specific strategies for differentiating feedback. Chapter 5 presents the idea of using a pathways tool for coaching collaborative teams to guide a team's conversations. While clarity and feedback are critical, nothing will happen without timely and targeted support that aligns with what the team needs to improve its practice.

Part III connects research and practice. Chapter 6 uses two real-life scenarios to illustrate how combining the concepts of clarity, feedback, and support can have a positive impact on collaborative teams' effectiveness. Finally, the afterword concludes our discussion of coaching collaborative teams in a PLC, identifying the powerful possibilities this kind of a shift can have on teaching and learning.

A Comprehensive Approach

We want to be clear that shifting the focus from coaching individual teachers to coaching collaborative teams does not mean that districts should abandon their traditional instructional coaching models. We do not advocate choosing between coaching individual teachers *or* collaborative teams; we advocate coaching for individual teachers *and* collaborative teams. Coaching is not an either-or proposition. We believe the development of different approaches to coaching that are focused on improving the daily performance of collaborative teams is necessary and needs to become a higher priority.

Some will suggest our framework is nothing new. We agree that much of the kind of coaching we envision does combine many aspects of several different coaching models. We have made no attempt to repackage the work of dedicated coaches and practitioners into a new model of coaching. Our interest is in moving from best practice to next practice using what we already know about coaching and collaboration with a conscious and intentional focus on ensuring that collaborative teacher teams fully implement PLC practices.

What *is* different is our belief that a shift in focus from coaching individual teachers to coaching collaborative teams is timely and beneficial. The rationale for this shift is simple: if coaching individuals is good, then coaching collaborative teams is better.

PART I

THE WHY, HOW, AND WHAT OF COACHING COLLABORATIVE TEAMS

CHAPTER 1

Combining Collaboration and Coaching

Research findings indicate that effective coaching structures promote a collaborative culture where large numbers of school personnel feel ownership and responsibility for leading improvement efforts in teaching and learning.

—ANNENBERG INSTITUTE FOR SCHOOL REFORM

Collaboration and coaching are familiar concepts in schools. There is a considerable body of anecdotal and empirical evidence that show both have a positive impact on teaching and learning. However, these two powerful concepts remain largely independent from one another within the context of improving schools. We believe it is time to re-examine the traditional perspective on both coaching and collaboration in order to amplify the effect each can have on teaching and learning.

When implementing a new teaching strategy or curriculum, teachers often seek out colleagues and form informal coaching relationships. In creating these ad hoc, sometimes impromptu partnerships, "They seek out relationships with more knowledgeable or experienced colleagues to ask advice, model lessons, or start an inquiry group" (Yang, 2016, p. 50). Schools can capitalize on teachers' natural inclination to work together by creating formal coaching structures that support the work of collaborative teams within PLCs.

This chapter examines collaboration and coaching as separate constructs and then explores the potentially powerful and practical impact coaching can have on collaborative teams in a PLC. To begin, we review the research that supports teacher collaboration.

Collaboration

According to Eaker and Dillard (2017), "There is a strong body of evidence that teacher collaboration can positively affect student achievement" (p. 46). Widely recognized as an essential element of an effective school, collaboration and collaborative teaming has been called "the single most important factor for successful [school] restructuring" (Eastwood & Louis, 1992, p. 215) and "the key to ensuring that every child has a quality teacher" (National Commission on Teaching and America's Future [NCTAF], 2003, p. 7).

Education researcher J. W. Little (1990) identifies five specific benefits of collaboration, stating:

> When teachers work in collaborative teams, schools are more likely to see gains in student achievement, find higher quality solutions to problems, promote increased confidence among staff, create an environment in which teachers support one another's strengths and accommodate weakness, and provide support for new ideas, materials, and methods. (as cited in DuFour, 2010, p. 153)

Researchers also identify other benefits of collaboration. "Teacher collaboration in strong professional learning communities improves the quality and equity of student learning, promotes discussions that are grounded in evidence and analysis rather than opinion, and fosters collective responsibility for student success" (McLaughlin & Talbert (2006), as cited in DuFour, 2010 p. 154).

Additionally, collaboration has a positive effect on a school's professional practice. According to Mona Mourshed, Chinezi Chijioke, and Michael Barber (2010) (as cited in DuFour, 2010):

> The high-performing systems we studied had strong routines of collaborative practice. This collaboration made teaching public and fostered shared responsibility for student learning. There was a move away from an emphasis on what was taught towards an emphasis on what students learned. Teachers became more reflective about and more knowledgeable of good teaching practice. (p. 155)

Researchers point to mounting evidence showing the importance of educators working collaboratively in a PLC because professional communities are "related to improved instruction, student achievement, and one of our leadership variables (shared leadership)" (Louis, Leithwood, Wahlstrom, & Anderson, 2010, p. 42).

Carrie R. Leana (2011) finds "a significant correlation between student learning growth and school environments where positive collaborations flourished" (as cited in Basileo, 2016, p. 3). Lindsey Devers Basileo (2016), senior research analyst at Learning Sciences International, notes that collaboration benefits students and teachers alike: "a high level of teacher collaboration significantly improves student achievement," and "PLCs that examine student work and analyze student data more frequently are likely to have higher levels of teacher morale" (p. 1).

Despite overwhelming support for collaboration, school professionals still work in isolation. This condition is more about what schools *don't do* than any conscious effort to make it difficult for teachers to collaborate. The problem is many structures that currently exist in schools conspire against teachers working together.

For example, examine the master schedule in most schools. The traditional schedule provides very little time for teachers to meet and collaborate during the regular school day. Schools often relegate conversations about teaching and learning to lunchtime or before and after school, some of the least productive time for collaboration. Schools that are serious about fostering collaboration and transforming into PLCs must begin to designate and protect time during the regular school day for teacher teams to meet; this sacred time is essential.

Even the time-honored blueprint of a traditional school building reinforces working in isolation. All one has to do is look at the physical layout of schools, with individual classrooms housing individual teachers along either side of a long hallway. As Kathleen Fulton, Irene Yoon, and Christine Lee (2005) state, "It is time to end the practice of solo teaching in isolated classrooms" (p. 4). Kathleen Fulton and Ted Britton (2011) add:

> To meet the needs of today's learners, the tradition of artisan teaching and solo-practice classrooms will have to give way to a school culture in which teachers continuously develop their content knowledge and pedagogical skills through collaborative practice that is embedded in the daily fabric of their work. (p. 5)

Eaker and Dillard (2017) report that "achievement gains were greater in schools with strong collaborative environments and in the classrooms of teachers who were strong collaborators" (p. 47). When teachers collaborate in teams within a PLC, they improve their practice in two important ways: (1) they share specific instructional strategies for teaching more effectively, and (2) they deepen their content knowledge by identifying the specific standards students must master. In other words, when teachers work together they become better teachers.

Not only do teachers who work on collaborative teams improve the quality of their instructional practice, they improve it more rapidly. Eaker and Dillard (2017) cite evidence that "a teacher's rate of improvement increased when working in schools with better collaboration as compared to working in schools with ineffective collaboration" (p. 47).

Working collaboratively with other teachers is far more effective than working in isolation, but the truth is, most teachers spend the school day working alone. They routinely find themselves in classrooms filled with students but void of any other adults. Popular culture has celebrated the individual teacher who, working alone and despite significant obstacles and challenges, inspires students to excel and achieve far beyond anyone's expectations. This narrative, while celebrated in popular films such as *Dangerous Minds* and *Freedom Writers*, does not always reflect reality. As we've noted, research shows that a shift to celebrating the collective achievements of collaborative teams of teachers within PLCs would better serve educators.

What is clear from the research is that the act of collaborating with colleagues improves the quality of a teacher's instructional practice. As Tom Carroll (2009), president emeritus of the National Commission on Teaching and America's Future, maintains, "Quality teaching is not an individual accomplishment, it is the result of a collaborative culture that empowers teachers to team up to improve student learning beyond what any one of them can achieve alone" (p. 13).

Coaching

Educators acknowledge that coaching is an effective way to improve a teacher's instructional practice, and many agree with Matthew Kraft, David Blazer, and Dylan Hogan (2017), who suggest coaching is a "key lever for improving teachers' classroom instruction and for translating knowledge into classroom practices" (p. 7). Though pervasive and widespread, most support for coaching thus far has come in the form of testimony or anecdotal commentary from practitioners. The Annenberg Institute for School Reform (2004) notes that "as coaching is a relatively new approach to instructional capacity building, there is increasing demand for evidence that it [coaching] improves teaching practice and increases student learning" (p. 6).

Sebastian Wren and Diana Vallejo (2009) acknowledge the limited state of the coaching literature but are optimistic that "as more empirical evidence about instructional coaching as a model for professional development becomes available, there will be more evidence based consensus about the most effective roles and practices for professionals in this position" (p. 2). Despite the lack of empirical evidence, few practitioners disagree about the positive impact effective coaching programs can have on teaching and learning.

Bruce Joyce and Beverly Showers "conducted, possibly, the best-known studies that show the positive effects of coaching" (Killion & Harrison, 2017, p. 11). Killion and Harrison (2017) report:

> In multiple studies of professional development programs in several school districts across the country, Joyce and Showers (1995) found that when presentation of theory, demonstration, and low-risk practice were combined with coaching and other forms of follow-up support, such as study groups, teachers' use of instructional strategies increased dramatically. (p. 11)

Killion and Harrison (2007) continue, "Since their initial study in 1980, subsequent studies have consistently found that teachers' implementation of new learning rises dramatically when peer coaching sessions occur" (p. 12).

In their research, Joyce and Showers (1985) demonstrate that the traditional forms of professional development (the large-group, one-size-fits-all training sessions that experts deliver—including those experts that make an effort to include opportunities for modeling and practice) are insufficient to ensure the successful implementation of new ideas. Coached teachers are more likely to understand the purpose of a new strategy, use the new strategy more frequently with greater skill, and experience more successful implementation of the new strategy than uncoached teachers who attend the identical professional development. Absent the coaching component in their professional development experience, teachers are less likely to incorporate new teaching strategies into their classroom routines and repertoire.

Joyce and Showers's (2002) research shows that professional development that includes discussions of the *why* and *what* of a new idea or technique, coupled with demonstration and practice of the strategy during the training, has little impact on a teacher's routine practice. It is not until schools or districts add coaching to the training experience that teachers are able to routinely transfer the new knowledge, skills, and dispositions into their teaching repertoires.

They also find that coaching promotes larger, more systemic benefits. Coaching promotes the development of a common language and shared knowledge, adherence to professional norms, and a commitment to continuous improvement. In short, coaching promotes many key elements of highly effective PLCs. Table 1.1 (page 16) summarizes Joyce and Showers's (2002) findings.

Table 1.1: Training Components and Attainment of Outcomes

Components	Knowledge	Skill	Transfer (Executive Implementation)
	Percent of Participants Who Attained Outcomes		
Study of Theory	10	5	0
Demonstrations	30	20	0
Practice	60	60	5
Coaching	95	95	95

Source: Joyce and Showers, 2002.

Beth Boatright and Chrysan Gallucci's (2008) observations align with the findings of Joyce and Showers as well as those of a host of other researchers who argue that coaching benefits educators in many ways. Coaching:

- Encourages actively reflecting on current practices (Garmston, Linder, & Whitaker, 1993; Joyce & Showers, 1982; Stein & D'Amico, 2002)

- Informs teachers how to apply new concepts to their unique work environments (Neufeld & Roper, 2003; Showers & Joyce, 1996)

- Builds generative communities of practice (McKinney & Lowenhaupt, 2007; Showers, 1985)

- Fosters professionalism among colleagues (Boatright, Gallucci, Swanson, Van Lare, & Yoon, 2008; Garmston, 1987; Perkins, 1998)

The use of traditional instructional coaching models in education is quite high, but traditional coaching may not generate the kinds of results school leaders are looking for. Sebastian Wren and Diana Vallejo (2009) note that there is mounting (albeit tangential) evidence that there are problems with traditional coaching in schools across the United States. Barbara Neufeld and Dana Roper (2003) report that "coaching models that rely solely on one-on-one interactions between the coach and the teacher do not show as much promise as those that incorporate small-group [team] learning" (p. 20).

Best Practice Versus Next Practice

Many districts employ coaching models that are *teaching centric*. In these models, coaching is delivered to teachers individually and is focused on improving an individual teacher's performance on a specific set of instructional skills or curricula. The coaching is voluntary, delivered in a one-on-one setting, and is typically based on a teacher's request or, occasionally, feedback from a coach or evaluator. These traditional coaching models tend to rely heavily on the teachers' and coaches' perceptions as the measure of effectiveness.

Other coaching models, such as one from the Public Education & Business Coalition (PEBC; www.pebc.org), embrace a more calibrated and systemic view of best practice. While these models continue the practice of providing support through one-on-one relationships and focus on improving specific instructional strategies or understanding new curricula, they provide feedback anchored to an agreed-on standard of best practice—some kind of rubric or continuum that tracks the teacher's growth and progress. When teachers work with coaches from PEBC (2012), they choose from seven categories and thirty-six subcomponents of the PEBC Continuum of Growth in Best Instructional Practices (PEBC, 2012) to self-assess their progress. The coaching occurs with the goal of moving teachers from one level of expertise to the next. Support is based on a teacher's needs or interests, and while these models offer more consistent measures of effectiveness, individual teachers typically work with a coach in settings that are separate and apart from colleagues who teach the same class, course, or grade level.

A few highly successful schools and districts, such as Kildeer Countryside Community Consolidated School District 96 in Buffalo Grove, Illinois, and the Cherry Creek School District in Greenwood Village, Colorado, have begun exploring models that prioritize coaching collaborative teams. Their approach also incorporates a rubric, continuum, or strategy implementation guide to describe the practices teachers must engage in to improve. Teachers continue to help identify the content coaches will work on, but the topics reflect the team's consensus. Furthermore, all team members receive coaching simultaneously in a one-on-many setting.

In contrast to traditional instructional coaching models, team-orientated coaching is *learning centric*, grounded in collaborative team structures, and supported with a proven model of school improvement (the PLC process). This approach uses coaching resources more efficiently, and measures of effectiveness are based on the results of valid and reliable assessments of student learning.

Table 1.2 (page 18) identifies some differences between traditional coaching models and an approach to coaching that focuses on supporting collaborative teams.

Table 1.2: Differences Between Coaching Individual Teachers and Coaching Teams

Coaching Individual Teachers	Coaching Teacher Teams
Encourages working in isolation	Encourages working collaboratively
Limits access to resources and expertise	Expands access to resources and expertise
Aims to fix individual teacher's deficits	Aims to build on a collaborative team's assets
Uses perceptions to measure growth	Uses assessment results to measure growth
Promotes individual improvement	Promotes collective improvement
Is more resource and cost intensive	Is more resource and cost efficient

To begin making the case for coaching collaborative teams, we will compare and contrast some of the differences, both positive and negative, between the traditional coaching models focused on supporting individual teachers and models that prioritize the coaching of collaborative teams.

Isolation Versus Collaboration

An unintended consequence of traditional instructional coaching models is that they encourage teachers to work in isolation. Conventional instructional coaching models rely on one-on-one relationships between the coach and teacher as opposed to a team approach, which capitalizes on the one-on-many structure or teams. Coaching individual teachers on discrete and often isolated instructional practices makes it difficult for teachers to collaborate. It is virtually impossible for a grade-level or departmental team to set common goals, share resources, or leverage the synergy that comes from collaborating if each team member works independently to improve a different instructional strategy. Coaching teams encourages just the opposite and allows teachers to leverage the many benefits that come from working collaboratively with their peers. As Neufeld and Roper (2003) report, "In addition to increased efficiency afforded by small groups [collaborative teams], such interactions between teachers and coaches lead more quickly to the development of instructionally focused school cultures" (p. 20).

Limited Versus Expanded Access to Resources and Expertise

Another outcome of traditional coaching models is that the one-on-one relationship between a coach and an individual teacher may actually limit a teacher's access to the expertise he or she needs to improve. Working in isolation restricts the expertise a teacher can access to the knowledge base of the coach and any resources that particular coach may be able to bring to the instructional practice the individual teacher is working to improve. The obvious problem is that no single individual has all the knowledge, skills, and experience every situation needs. In a team setting, the other team members' experience and perspectives multiply the coach's expertise. Instead of responding to suggestions a single coach generates, teachers working to improve their practice benefit from the feedback they receive from the coach *and* their colleagues. These types of small-group settings "allow teachers to learn in collaboration with one another and with the coach" (Neufeld & Roper, 2003, p. 9).

A Deficit Versus an Asset Orientation

A liability of traditional instructional coaching models is their deficit orientation; these models focus on correcting some aspect of a teacher's instructional practice that needs improvement—often those a coach or administrator identifies. Education consultant Diane Sweeney (2011) finds that "this approach doesn't take us very far and only serves to divide a school culture into those who are 'doing it' and those that aren't" (p. 179).

Coaching teams shifts the emphasis from fixing an individual's deficits to building on the assets of teams to generate new approaches or solutions to problems. Teachers working collaboratively "apply their learning more deeply, frequently, and consistently than teachers working alone" (Annenberg Institute for School Reform, 2004, p. 2).

Perception Versus Results

The traditional coaching models use an individual teacher's perceptions to measure the growth of the teacher involved in the process. Sometimes determining whether or not the teacher has improved relies on an agreed-on standard of best practice, and sometimes it hinges on the perceptions of the coach or the individual teacher. This is in contrast to a team-coaching approach where common assessment data measure growth in a team's overall instructional effectiveness.

Individual Versus Collective Improvement

Traditional coaching models improve teacher effectiveness one teacher at a time. Coaching collaborative teams improves teacher effectiveness several teachers at a time. Thus, coaching teams instead of individuals "exponentially increas[es] the impact of coaching so that more teachers benefit from the coaching provided" (Killion, Harrison, Bryan, & Clifton, 2012, p. 160).

Resource and Cost Intensive Versus Resource and Cost Efficient

Traditional instructional coaching models built around one-on-one relationships between coaches and teachers can be resource and cost intensive. It can be difficult to build a rationale to increase the number of coaches when budgets are tight. Jim Knight (2012) estimates the per-teacher cost of traditional coaching to range from "$3,300 to upwards of $5,200" (as cited in Kraft et al., 2017, p. 27). However, shifting to a model that emphasizes coaching teams can mitigate those cost concerns by multiplying the impact of a coach from a single teacher to multiple teachers while accomplishing the same goals—and perhaps produce even better results.

A Practical Shift

Perhaps the most persuasive argument we can make for coaching collaborative teams instead of individual teachers is a practical one: coaching teams is a more effective and efficient way to improve schools. Whether they are working with collaborative teams or individual teachers, coaches have the same goal: to improve teachers' instructional practice, thereby positively impacting student learning. As Joellen Killion (2012), senior advisor at Learning Forward, and her colleagues point out, "Team coaching intends to move information into practice, just as one-on-one coaching does. Working one-on-one is a less efficient way, however, to make a substantive difference for teachers and students" (p. 159).

In spite of the many benefits of coaching, some schools and districts argue they simply cannot afford coaches. If they do employ coaches, they often do so on a limited basis, allocating their coaching resources to a small number of beginning teachers or experienced teachers performing at marginal levels. This approach creates several issues for principals.

First, targeting a limited group of teachers ignores the benefits coaching can have for *all* teachers and the systemwide impact. Even the most experienced teachers can learn new strategies and curricula. Second, rationing scarce coaching resources to support a limited number of teachers ignores the powerful potential of building teachers' capacity to help one another. Traditional models of coaching reinforce working in isolation, which is one of the reasons so many new teachers leave the profession during the first five years of their career. Jeffery Mirel and Simona Goldin (2012) report that researchers from the Gates Foundation "found that nearly 90 percent of U.S. teachers believe that providing time to collaborate with colleagues is crucial to retaining good teachers." Shifting the focus of coaching from individuals to teams addresses all these concerns. It allows schools to achieve a systematic impact and build capacity among the entire staff.

Achieving a Systemwide Impact

Another practical element in the shift from coaching individual teachers to coaching collaborative teams is that the number of coaches available to work with individual teachers is usually inadequate to create the kind of systemwide impact necessary to successfully implement new initiatives. While one can reasonably expect a coach in a traditional coaching model to support a handful of individual teachers, a coach's impact within a framework that emphasizes coaching teams is much greater; it is simple mathematics. It is challenging for coaches to support more than six or eight individual teachers at any one time, but if that same coach works with six or eight teams, he or she would impact twenty or thirty teachers. Given the same amount of time, a coach's impact is potentially far greater when the focus is on teams instead of individuals.

Building Capacity With Collaboration

Another practical result of the shift to coaching collaborative teams is the ability to build capacity. There will inevitably be times when teachers need help and the coach is not available. The solution to this dilemma is to build team members' capacity to help one another. When schools use a team approach to coaching:

> Team members learn about their colleagues' strengths and explore how others think about teaching. They become more interdependent. They build the capacity to support one another over time when the coach is not available, and so long-term change becomes more sustainable. (Killion et al., 2012, p. 160)

Coaching teams builds the team members' capacity to support each other, and in the event that problems arise when the coach is unavailable, teachers can turn to their colleagues for help. Plus, research suggests that collaborating with (talking to) peers about instructing students is a critical part of a teacher's job and results in higher student achievement (Leana, 2011). Leana (2011) studied teacher effectiveness in more than one thousand classrooms. She asked teachers where they went most often to find answers to questions about their own practice. She did not find that teachers cited workshops or working with external consultants as their top choice. Nor did they indicate that articles or research journals were particularly helpful. The teachers also acknowledged that they did not seek help from district-level curriculum experts or their principals. They didn't even mention popular internet resources like Pinterest or Teachers Pay Teachers as the best source of new ideas. Citing Leana's (2011) research, Basileo (2016) reports that "a teacher is, in fact, most likely to gather her knowledge about teaching from fellow teachers" (p. 3).

Leana (2011) reports that teachers are twice as likely to ask peers for help than to ask experts within their school district, such as content and curriculum coordinators. They are four times more likely to seek advice from a peer than from the principal.

These findings have significant implications for those seeking to improve their schools. If colleagues are a teacher's primary source of ideas to improve his or her instructional practice, it seems clear that:

> A high functioning PLC focused on the right work will act, in essence, as a kind of knowledge-generating system for teachers, where the effect of professional development is accelerated and refined through collective focus on learning within the teams. (Basileo, 2016, p. 3)

In light of this insight, schools must recognize that teams, not individuals, represent the best opportunity to improve teaching and learning. Those schools without coaching programs should start by creating structures to support the coaching of collaborative teams. Those with fully functioning instructional coaching models should redirect their coaching resources to improving the productivity of collaborative teams rather than individual teachers.

From Fixing to Cultivating

Not long ago, the textbook was the curriculum, there were no standards to guide the work, and teacher intuition determined evidence of progress. Districts hired specialists who focused on developing expertise in specific content areas to respond to this situation. The emphasis of the curriculum specialists' work was on improving a teacher's understanding of curriculum, which, theoretically, improved a teacher's instructional practice and the level of student achievement.

While principals reminded the faculty, "You teach students, not content," curriculum coordinators were encouraged to do just the opposite; they focused on coaching content and curriculum, not teachers. Perhaps it should have been obvious at the time, but what no one seemed to recognize was that content expertise was of little value if that expertise remained within the purview of a limited number of district curriculum coordinators or a few teachers on district-level curriculum committees.

Schools have changed a lot. Teachers now view textbooks as a resource to support the curriculum; standards help identify what all students should know and be able to do; and evidence of growth relies on results from a combination of local, state or province, and national assessments. The focus of coaching has also changed. The emphasis has shifted from enhancing a teacher's content expertise to improving a teacher's instructional practice.

Let's be clear, content and curricular expertise are important—at the team level. It matters very little if that expertise remains cloistered amongst a few experts at the district level. It makes far more sense for content specialists and curriculum coordinators to shift their attention from coaching content to coaching teams.

According to Laura Desimone and Katie Pak (2017), "Focusing on content and/or how students learn that content is an important dimension of effective PD [professional development]" (p. 5). They cite evidence that "when PD [professional development] is integrated explicitly into teachers' daily instructional routines, it is more likely to be effective" (p. 8). Desimone and Pak (2017) continue:

> The presence of a coach [content specialist or curricular coordinator] in these grade-level meetings is useful when teachers look for expert opinion in navigating the technical challenges of implementing new instructional approaches or in gaining deeper understanding of ways to reconstruct their practice. (p. 7)

Killion and her colleagues (2012) agree: "Learning a new skill is macro-learning that often occurs in more formal professional learning such as a workshop. However, learning does not become useful or valuable until it is transferred into practice" (p. 163). The role of the content expert is critical, and individuals with a thorough understanding of particular content areas have tremendous value if, and it is a big if, they are able to transfer their expertise to the team level.

The goal of those with content and curricular expertise must be to support development of collaborative teams. Teachers do not need another list, guide, handbook, or overview. Those with specific content knowledge can help teams prioritize standards, identify learning targets, and craft student-friendly *I can* statements. The knowledge of specific content is also very beneficial when teams are developing common assessments or creating success criteria and learning progressions.

To maximize their impact on student learning, content and curriculum coordinators must find ways to transfer their content knowledge to collaborative teams at the building level. Yes, teachers need coaches who know that good curriculum matters; however, they must recognize that good instruction matters more. We understand all too well that "good teaching can overcome poor curriculum, but good curriculum cannot overcome poor teaching" (Marzano, 2017).

There is widespread, nearly universal agreement that coaching improves a teacher's instructional practice. We acknowledge that teachers benefit from intensive support and agree that providing one-to-one coaching has been an effective way to differentiate professional development. Just as widely accepted is the notion that working collaboratively is more effective than working in isolation. In education, we agree on the fact that collaboration is not an optional activity—it is an expectation.

As Diane Sweeney (2011) suggests, up until now, most traditional coaching models have focused on 'fixing' a teacher's deficiencies rather than cultivating learning. We agree with Sweeney's assessment and believe it's time to shift the focus of traditional coaching models. If schools are to continue improving, they must begin to transition from the current practice of coaching individual teachers on a discreet set of instructional strategies, skills, or curricula to an expanded vision of coaching collaborative teams within PLCs to improve their PLC practices.

Sweeney (2011) recommends that schools begin this transition "by focusing coaching on specific goals for student learning, rather than on changing or fixing teachers" and then "navigat[ing] directly towards a measurable impact and increased student achievement" (p. 1). This subtle but powerful shift in focus closely aligns with one of the most important tenets of the PLC model—the belief that learning, not teaching, is a school's fundamental purpose.

Conclusion

We can accomplish more when we work together. Our notion of teaming in schools has evolved from groups of individuals cooperating and coordinating when convenient to a very intentional, purposeful, and conscious effort to improve our practice by collaborating with others. There is plenty of evidence of the real benefits of collaboration. Killion and Harrison (2017) point out that "collaboration among teachers builds capacity and reduces variance in the quality of teaching across classrooms within a school" (p. 161). They argue that collaboration also promotes "a culture of continuous improvement and collective responsibility for the success of every student and educator within a school" (p. 161). The evolution of our collaborative practice has meant that students and adults alike are better off now that the idea of working with others is both an accepted *and* expected way of "doing school."

We also accomplish more with the help of a coach. Whether at work or play, at home or school, a good coach celebrates when we succeed and supports us when we struggle. Coaches highlight our strengths, bring out our best, and help us achieve more than we thought possible. And, there is a growing body of evidence that coaching has a positive impact on schools. Killion and Harrison (2017) believe that much like collaboration, coaching can also "contribute to shifting the culture within a school to one that is more collaborative, supportive, and transparent" (p. 203). Coaching and collaboration go hand in hand.

Killion, Harrison, Bryan, and Clifton (2009) illustrate why coaching collaborative teams is more effective and efficient than current practice. One reason is because "coaches who work with teams give teachers the opportunity to engage with multiple thinking partners rather than one" (p. 160). They argue that "changing teaching and student learning takes time yet the speed of change can be accelerated when coaches work at least part of their day with teams of teachers" (p. 162).

Perhaps Ann Delehant (2006; cited in Killion & Harrison, 2017) explains best why schools should shift from coaching individuals to coaching teams when she observes:

> We've become more aware of the power of team coaching. Teams can achieve results when coaches spend time with them to: a) use data and student work to align instruction and assessments; b) coordinate peer visits, organize and support grade-level and department teams; c) facilitate professional learning; and build a more collaborative culture in every school. (p. 170)

Delehant (2006) concludes by saying, "We have great success when coaches work with individuals, but we go farther faster when we work with teams" (as cited in Killian & Harrison, p. 170).

This chapter built the rationale for coaching collaborative teams. Just as we believe that all students can learn to high levels, so too do we believe that all teams can collaborate at high levels. And just as all students don't learn in the same way or at the same time and some will need additional time and support to succeed, some teams will need additional time and support to become high-performing collaborative teams. It is the act of differentiating, of meeting teams where they are, that makes the notion of coaching collaborative teams so compelling. In the next chapter, we connect the idea of the act of coaching collaborative teams to the PLC process.

CHAPTER 2

Coaching Collaborative Teams in a PLC

A well-designed and supported coaching program weds the core elements of effective professional development with the essential goals of professional learning communities in ways that advance both school and systemic improvement.

—ANNENBERG INSTITUTE FOR SCHOOL REFORM

At their core, educators are driven to make a difference and provide students with productive options beyond their high school years. Many school and district leaders select the PLC model as the major improvement initiative for their school. Some have come to this decision after years of struggle with lower-than-expected levels of student achievement. Others enter this work knowing most of their students are already achieving at high levels. Regardless of their student-achievement scores or demographics, these schools commit to learning for all—whatever it takes (DuFour et al., 2016).

When we, as a staff, commit to learning for all, we agree to take collective responsibility for all students, no matter what their circumstances. We commit to the uncomfortable work of being self-reflective and changing our practice to become a more productive collaborative team. More productive teams lead to better teachers, and better teachers lead to increased student achievement.

One method for strengthening collaborative teams is through coaching. A well-trained coach, whether a principal, a lead teacher, or an outside consultant, has the opportunity to nudge teams toward accomplishing the mission and vision of their school by teaching them how to engage in the practices of a PLC. It is important, however, that these coaches fully understand the premises of a PLC and that there is a common understanding among leaders about the future they are trying to create. In the next section, we discuss the basics of PLCs and explain ways we believe coaches can enhance PLC practices. (For an in-depth examination of the PLC process, we recommend the foundational resource *Learning By Doing: A Handbook for Professional Learning Communities at Work*, 3rd edition [DuFour et al., 2016].)

Three Big Ideas of a PLC

Three big ideas form the basis for a PLC: (1) a focus on learning, (2) a collaborative culture, and (3) a results orientation (DuFour et al., 2016). Let's begin by looking at the first big idea.

A Focus on Learning

It may seem obvious that teachers should focus on student learning rather than on teaching as the fundamental purpose of a school, but a bit of honest reflection on practice shows that many teachers still focus more on instruction than on whether or not students have learned. Teachers feel pressure to cover the curriculum; but there is a difference between covering the curriculum and teaching the curriculum. If the emphasis is on coverage, there is often little regard for how much of that material students actually learn.

Even teams in high-performing PLCs can get stuck on teaching. Parry Graham and William Ferriter (2008) observe, "Unless challenged, team attention remains centered on teaching rather than learning. School leaders must ask teams to answer basic questions about outcomes" (p. 39). Graham and Ferriter (2008) go on to say that leaders should act as coaches, "serving as collaborative partners in ongoing conversations about teaching and learning" (p. 42). In other words, coaches (whether they be administrators, teacher leaders, outside consultants, or other types of coaches) should be intentionally helping teams maintain their focus on student learning.

A Collaborative Culture

The second big idea of a PLC is a collaborative culture in which team members work together interdependently to achieve a common goal or goals for which they are mutually accountable (DuFour et al., 2016). As mentioned previously, traditionally, teaching has been an act that an individual teacher performs in isolation. For teachers to be successful working in collaborative teams, they need the opportunity to develop a range of competencies and skills that relate to creating a collaborative culture.

We know that coaching collaborative teams promotes positive cultural change. Researchers point to the fact that "[high-achieving schools] build a school environment where working together to solve problems and to learn from each other become cultural norms" (WestEd, 2000, p. 12) and that "the conditions, behaviors, and practices required by an effective coaching program can [positively] affect the culture of a school or system" (Annenberg Institute for School Reform, 2004, p. 2). In addition to the positive impact coaching collaborative teams has on school culture, research indicates that effective coaching promotes "a collaborative culture where large numbers of school personnel feel ownership and responsibility for leading improvement efforts in teaching and learning" (Annenberg Institute for School Reform, 2004, p. 4).

Most teachers have had very little exposure to working collaboratively with other teachers, and building this kind of a skill set doesn't happen without some guidance. When we simply assume that teachers can work effectively in collaborative teams without guidance, we may be expecting too much of them. Fostering a robust PLC requires conscious steps toward developing the capacity of teachers to collaborate effectively. Coaches can make an enormous contribution to this work.

For example, coaches can assist teams starting their PLC transformation. Teams might need guidance in the four pillars of a PLC—shared (1) mission, (2) vision, (3) values (collective commitments), and (4) goals—or with establishing norms for group participation, building high levels of trust, defining roles and responsibilities, and reaching consensus. Coaches can help teams:

- Identify SMART goals (O'Neill & Conzemius, 2005, 2014)—
  - **S**trategic and specific
  - **M**easurable
  - **A**ttainable
  - **R**esults oriented
  - **T**ime bound
- Experience protocols
- Maintain a team's focus on the right work

Even in schools in which a collaborative culture exists, conflict among team members does arise. Coaches can help teams move past conflict. Because of their strong interpersonal skills and the trust that they have with individual teachers, coaches can bring team members together who might otherwise struggle to mesh. For example, coaches often have experience with techniques such as cognitive coaching and conflict resolution, which can bring team members to a place of common understanding and agreement that helps them work together toward team goals, despite their differences. This helps teams develop a sense of collective responsibility—a PLC hallmark—where all teachers invest in the success of the students, their colleagues, and the school as a whole (DuFour et al., 2016). When all staff members truly invest, achievement increases.

According to Kent Peterson (2002), "School culture is a set of norms, values and beliefs, celebrations and ceremonies, symbols and stories, that make up the 'persona' of a school" (2002b, p. 10). Teacher teams can only function within a PLC when they are operating within a culture that values and promotes collaboration. In order to be effective, teams must have regularly scheduled collaboration time during which they explicitly communicate the expected products from that work. While this collaborative culture needs to permeate the entire school, coaches can work with individual grade-level or content-area teams to develop the positive relationships and trust among members that must be present for teams to truly be collaborative.

A Results Orientation

PLCs have a *results orientation*—the third big idea (DuFour et al., 2016). Team members are constantly seeking evidence of the results they desire—high levels of student learning. Members of collaborative teams use evidence as part of a continuous-improvement process that aims to improve results for individual teachers, for the team, and for the school. As a means of making sure students are on the right track and progressing toward desired levels of proficiency, effective teams regularly measure their students' progress through common assessments (both formative, assessment *for* learning, and summative, assessment *of* learning). However, regular measurement alone does nothing to improve results; it is only the action educators take through results analysis that truly leads to improved achievement.

Teams may not understand data's relevance or how they can use data to improve teaching and learning. Many teams spend the majority of their meeting time calculating data and very little time connecting the results back to their own instruction. With these teams, there are few discussions about what these data truly reveal about student mastery or how to improve learning. When these teams have coaches, however, the tenor of these meetings changes. Coaches help teams move beyond calculation toward reflection on what their students learn and how their instruction may impact student learning. Most important, coaches can help teachers use results to determine next steps for instruction, intervention, and enrichment.

While some teachers have difficulty using student data, other teachers simply do not want to. Data and what they reveal may threaten teachers. In some cases, teachers are afraid school leaders and others will use assessment results against them. However, educators are working in an age of accountability and cannot hide from results. When coaches have a trusting relationship with teams, they can show members how to take control of their own data and use them as a tool to improve teaching and learning.

There are certain conditions that must be in place if teams are going to be a safe place where teachers can effectively analyze and utilize student data. Amanda Datnow and Vicki Park (2015) identify five foundational components that will help teams achieve this.

1. Everyone on the team shares responsibility for all students.

2. Conversations about data include healthy disagreement.

3. Conversations about data engender trust rather than suspicion.

4. Teams must take a solution-oriented approach to data.

5. Teams must know what they're expected to accomplish with data.

Teams can't easily accomplish these components. Datnow and Park (2015) state that they require the support of leaders who must set the right tone and expectations for data use among teachers. As they note, "Leaders must create a culture of inquiry that allows for authentic teacher engagement in all stages of the data-use process" (p. 15).

Coaches are perfect for helping to set the right tone and expectations for using data. They can facilitate conversations with healthy disagreement that lead teams to a place of trust, respect, and understanding. Coaches can ensure that teams understand the goals of their meetings and the steps they need to take to attain them. They can provide teams with the structure for effective data conversations, while still allowing them the flexibility they need to explore and engage in collective inquiry. Research shows that:

> The likelihood of using new learning and sharing responsibility rises when colleagues guided by a coach, work together and hold each other accountable for improved teaching and learning (Barr, Simmons, & Sorrow, 2003; Collagens, Stoddard, & Cutler, 2003; WestEd, 2000). (Annenberg Institute for School Reform, 2004, p. 4)

When developing and sustaining a PLC, it is critical that coaches assist teams in maintaining their focus on learning, building a collaborative culture, and developing a results orientation. It is impossible for schools to develop into true PLCs without adopting these three big ideas.

In addition to supporting schools with the three big ideas of a PLC, coaches can provide support to forming or existing collaborative teams in responding to the four critical questions of a PLC.

The Four Critical Questions of a PLC

Richard DuFour, Rebecca DuFour, Robert Eaker, Thomas Many, and Mike Mattos (2016) identify the following four critical questions to which collaborative teacher teams within PLCs must respond:

1. What knowledge, skills, and dispositions should every student acquire as a result of this unit, course, or grade level?
2. How will we know when each student has acquired the essential knowledge and skills?
3. How will we respond when students do not learn?
4. How will we extend the learning for students who are already proficient? (p. 36)

A coach can work with grade-level or content-area teachers during team meetings to collectively respond to these four critical questions of learning. Teachers in PLCs engage in a collaborative process to clarify the knowledge, skills, and dispositions all students must acquire; monitor each student's learning on a timely basis; provide systematic, timely, and directive interventions when students don't learn; and develop strategies to enrich and extend the learning for students who are proficient. Most important, coaches ask thoughtful questions that require teachers to think deeply about their practice to identify what they can do to improve teaching and learning. The Annenberg Institute (2004) finds that "emerging evidence shows that teachers' success at changing (instructional) practice mirrors the work of the coaches" (p. 3).

Critical Question One

Coaches can help teams respond to the first critical question—What knowledge, skills, and dispositions should every student acquire as a result of this unit, this course, or this grade level?—so PLCs can determine how to equitably educate all students, no matter who happens to be their teacher. This means implementing a curriculum that is both guaranteed and viable—guaranteed because all students have an equal opportunity for learning and viable because it provides adequate time for teachers to teach content and for students to learn it (Marzano, 2003).

Stakeholders expect teachers to teach to a very large number of standards; however, there is no way that teachers can give all standards the same amount of time or emphasis. They must continually decide which standards to prioritize and what learning to target within the standards. In a PLC, teacher teams make those decisions collaboratively.

Teams work together to prioritize standards in regard to what degree each standard reflects the qualities of endurance, readiness, and leverage, and if a standard is likely to be on high-stakes assessments (Ainsworth, 2003). By prioritizing standards and creating a common pacing guide and scope and sequence, teams know how much time and emphasis to place on each standard and individual learning target. However, not all teachers feel prepared to do this kind of work. Teams that do not have members who fully understand the how and why of this process of prioritizing often flounder while trying to decide which standards take precedence over others. A coach who participates in this process can lead teams by asking thoughtful questions that require honest reflection, open dialogue, and eventually collaborative decision making that reflects team consensus.

Once they prioritize standards, coaches walk teams through the process of *unwrapping* standards to reveal individual learning targets (Ainsworth, 2003). This means breaking standards apart into their most basic components, skill by skill, so teams can intentionally focus their instruction and assessment on those specific targets. Coaches can help teams decide on a tentative pace for teaching these targets and design a scope and sequence that all team members can agree to deliver. A coach is the ideal person to support teams through this process by eliciting all team members' thoughts, experiences, and opinions.

A coach's participation in team meetings in which members decide on common instructional strategies is extremely valuable. Robert J. Marzano (2017) provides a good example of why we should coach teams when he observes that "a good teacher can overcome poor curriculum but good curriculum can never overcome poor teaching." Coaches also ensure teachers identify which strategies to use when they model these practices, coteach with team members, and observe teachers to provide them with feedback on their practice.

Critical Question Two

Coaches can also help teams respond to the second critical question—How will we know if each student has acquired the essential knowledge and skills?—so teachers can agree on a common definition of proficiency to determine precisely what it looks like when a student masters a target or standard.

Coaches can facilitate the conversation about proficiency so that team members hear all teacher voices and consider key elements of measuring proficiency, such as depth of knowledge and consistent methods of assessment. A coach asks probing questions and helps teams arrive at consensus. By specifically describing what constitutes proficiency, teams come to a common understanding on the end goal for student learning and can more intentionally plan their instruction as a means of reaching it.

Once the team defines proficiency, members collaboratively create common assessments to measure students' levels of proficiency. It is crucial that assessment items address the identified essential standards at the level of cognitive rigor expected for proficiency. Adding assessment items that measure at various levels of cognitive rigor will tell teachers exactly what levels of understanding students possess. Additionally, teams need to be intentional in the types of items with which they choose to measure student mastery. Whether teachers use constructed response, selected response, or performance tasks should depend on the skill they are assessing and the proficiency levels they expect for the essential standards. Even the distractors teachers include on assessments can profoundly influence the quality of information teams glean from the assessments.

Creating reliable and valid assessments is not a task with which all teachers are comfortable. While many item banks and premade assessments exist for teachers' use, experience shows that investment in the creation of assessments helps teachers become more intimately knowledgeable about their content and the assessment itself. Coaches who have a background in creating assessments can enhance the positive effects of teachers creating their own assessments. By guiding teams through the process of identifying and unwrapping essential standards, coming to a common understanding of what constitutes proficiency, and writing assessment items that align with the standards and desired levels of cognitive rigor, coaches can help improve the quality of assessments as well as data that teams derive from them.

Critical Question Three

Coaches can also help teams respond to the third critical question—How will we respond when some students do not learn?—to determine what interventions teachers can provide to students who struggle.

Analyzing common formative and summative assessment data involves some of the most important work teams within a PLC do. Only scrutinizing assessment results and student work can help teams truly understand exactly what students do and do not know. And only studying exactly what students do and do not know can help teams provide students who are struggling with the interventions they need to become successful.

In their study, Jason Brasel, Brette Garner, Britnie Delinger Kane, and Ilana Horn (2015) observed data teams. They find that most teams keep their conversations at the surface level of identifying what instructional interventions they should provide and to whom. Their goal was to move teams to what they call *responsive re-visioning*, a four-step process wherein teachers determine "what to reteach, how to reteach it, to whom it should be retaught, and why students struggled with the assessed content" (p. 4). They note that this four-step approach is the most likely to lead to instructional improvement.

Because teams tend to gravitate toward surface-level conversations, Brasel and his colleagues (2015) suggest that a coach or facilitator "push teachers' thinking" by using guiding questions and encouraging teachers to "dig deeper" (pp. 5–6). This is exactly the type of team coaching we recommend. Teams with access to a coach who has earned their trust and is able to respectfully challenge the team to take all four steps of responsive revisioning are almost certain to deepen their data-analysis conversations. Only then can teams identify students' weaknesses and collaboratively create intentional plans to intervene with students who are struggling. Whether it be through classroom interventions or by moving students through a pyramid of interventions, a multitiered system of support, or response to intervention system, it is imperative that we analyze data to identify the help our students need and provide it to them as quickly as possible.

Critical Question Four

Coaches can also help teams respond to the fourth and final critical question— How will we extend the learning for students who are already proficient?—to determine how to enrich the learning of students who show proficiency.

Teams often spend so much of their time focused on planning intervention for students who struggle that they do not address the needs of students who already demonstrate mastery of the standards. Teacher teams need to make time for these students and create plans that allow for enriched learning at higher levels of cognitive rigor and deeper application.

There are multiple points throughout each instructional unit at which teams may realize some of their students have already mastered the priority standards. For example, teams may analyze preassessment data to find they have students who have mastered a priority standard before instruction has even begun. It is important, then, that the team plans alternative instruction and assignments that challenge these students to stretch their thinking regarding the mastered standard, while simultaneously teaching the standard to the rest of the class. There may also be occasions where formative assessment data show a few students have mastered a standard during the expected time frame, while a majority of the students did not. Although the timing within the unit may be different, the team's response will be the same: provide students who have mastered the standard with meaningful enrichment activities while delivering additional instruction to the remaining students. As a final example, there have been times when a majority of students have shown mastery of a standard sooner than expected. In this case, teams may adjust their teaching plans so as not to waste valuable time teaching a topic that most students already know. They could simply teach that standard to the small group of students who have not mastered it, while providing the rest of the class with meaningful enrichment activities on the same standard.

Coaches can be instrumental in helping teams develop opportunities for students to stretch their thinking on essential standards. Designing instruction and activities at increased levels of cognitive rigor can be challenging, and teachers often confuse difficulty with rigor. For example, some teachers assign advanced students to read longer texts rather than assigning texts with higher complexity levels. They may also ask "nit-picky" questions about the details of a text rather than asking students to create an argument and justify it with evidence from the text. Coaches can act as sounding boards and provide teams with guidance when it comes to creating extension activities that require higher-order-thinking skills.

Coaches who utilize the four critical questions of a PLC to guide collaborative team meetings help ensure that team time is spent productively. Time is a human being's most valuable commodity, and most schools struggle to acquire time for teachers to collaborate on a regular basis. For schools that overcome those hurdles and obtain regular collaboration time, it is almost never enough. That being the case, teams must use every moment of collaborative team time to the greatest extent possible. Coaches can provide tools for guidance and support to keep teams focused on the right work.

Tools for Guidance and Support

It is unproductive for teachers in PLCs to spend precious collaborative team time discussing anything except student learning and teacher practices. However, team-meeting observations often reveal a loss of focus and what Richard DuFour calls *co-blab-oration* (DuFour et al., 2016), where team members may be talking to one another, but the conversation drifts away from student learning and teaching practices. When this occurs, teacher teams benefit from a coach's guidance and direction to keep their meetings on track.

Even teams that are able to keep their meetings focused on student learning and teacher practices benefit from a coach's guidance and direction. Sometimes there are gaps in teacher knowledge, and teams simply do not know what to do next. Caryn Wells and Linson Feun (2008) studied six schools that had been through nine days of professional development on the PLC model. They conducted interviews and made observations to determine which components of the PLC model the schools implemented and which they did not after three years. Their report finds that the culture had improved in the schools, but "not much progress [had been made] with regard to implementing the most important PLC concepts, such as analyzing and responding to student achievement, teacher learning, and developing shared practice based on best educational practice" (Wells & Feun, 2008, p. 49). During an interview, one educator said, "We don't have the skills or resources to dissect the learning. Where do we go?" (Wells & Feun, 2008, p. 50). While traditional professional development was helpful, it was not enough. These teams needed additional guidance to be successful.

There are many tools coaches can use to provide teams with guidance and support. One such tool is Pathways for Coaching Collaborative Teams (Thomas, 2016). This is a multipart tool based on the four critical questions of a PLC (DuFour et al., 2016). Each part consists of a series of cascading questions that lead teams through the process of analyzing student work and reflecting on their instructional practice. (See chapter 6, page 113, for more discussion of Pathways.) The pathways are designed to deepen thinking—to take teachers beyond surface-level conversations so that team members can truly learn from each other and from the data they are analyzing. They encourage change in practices that increase achievement, not just collaboration for the sake of improving school culture.

To illustrate the power of coaching collaborative teams using the pathways tool, we feature the following case study from East Detroit Public Schools in Michigan.

Case Study: East Detroit Public Schools

East Detroit Public Schools (renamed Eastpointe Community Schools in 2017) is a small district of about three thousand students located in southern Macomb County, Michigan. Since 2011, the district has been through some harrowing times. The recession of 2008 left East Detroit home values down more than 50 percent, which led to large-scale demographic shifts in the community. The once thriving city that attracted middle- and working-class families was now home to a significantly increased number of transient families living in poverty. The district soon encountered a $5 million financial deficit, declining enrollment, and plummeting student achievement. In order to combat the district's deficit, teachers took a 24 percent pay cut, and the district reduced operating expenses by more than 37 percent. These circumstances led to a mass exodus of teachers and students alike. By 2014, all four of the district's eligible schools were identified as priority, falling within the lowest 5 percent of schools in the state when measured by the state assessment. The Michigan School Reform Office was threatening the district with a takeover if it did not improve student achievement in short order. As part of its response, the district began its PLC journey with its two elementary schools. However, there was much groundwork to be laid. As a means of supporting East Detroit's quest to rapidly improve student achievement, the Macomb Intermediate School District assigned one of its consultants, Tesha Ferriby Thomas, to work with East Detroit administrators and teachers as a school-improvement facilitator. (The information and data in this case study and elsewhere in this book about East Detroit come from her work in the district. See also www.mischooldata.org for further information on East Detroit and Michigan schools.) Tesha's top priority was to help the staff build shared knowledge around the foundational philosophies of the PLC process as they began this work.

One of the first steps toward becoming a PLC was for staff to recognize the urgent need for change. Most understood the pressure they were receiving from the Michigan School Reform Office, but the most serious ramifications seemed to escape them. They did not truly and deeply understand that their success as teachers determined the lifelong success (or lack thereof) of their students. Many students entered the district years behind in their education, confronting traumatic issues outside of school that most people could not imagine. The staff needed a reminder of their original purpose for teaching.

The staff were asked to reflect honestly on the phrase familiar to PLCs—"All students can learn"—and what that truly means. They also took time to examine the school's mission and vision statements, two of the four pillars of a PLC (DuFour et al., 2016). Were teachers living that mission and vision every day? Each school created its own values (collective commitments)—the third pillar of a PLC and the guidelines by which the schools would abide in order to achieve their mission of improved student learning. The atmosphere of each school began to change as teachers learned to regularly ask themselves, "Does what I am doing align with our mission?"

These were important steps, but they were only the precursor to the work to come. Once a week, the entire teaching staff met for an hour before school to *learn by doing* (DuFour et al., 2016). Because reading is such a vital skill, the district decided to begin their PLC journey by focusing on reading instruction. To help them begin forming a guaranteed and viable reading curriculum, teachers worked in grade-level collaborative teams to identify priority standards using Ainsworth's (2003) test of endurance, readiness, and leverage and then unwrapped each priority standard using Kim Bailey and Chris Jakicic's (2012) unwrapping template. This process would help teams narrow the curriculum and focus on specific instructional targets, which all students would be expected to master. (Visit **go.SolutionTree.com/PLCbooks** to find a link to Bailey and Jakicic's [2012] unwrapping tool.)

The idea of focusing on fewer standards was a welcome one but was also scary for the teachers. What if they chose the wrong standards? What was it about the other standards that made them considered nonessential? Teams worked through these questions and concluded that it would benefit students more to master a smaller number of extremely important standards than to have a vague understanding of them all. The unwrapping process allowed teachers to see the multiple targets within an individual standard, which opened their eyes to the need for far more specificity and intentionality in their teaching. Teams completed a priority standard summary chart for each essential standard, which included student *I can* statements, a definition of proficiency, and necessary vocabulary and prerequisite skills. (See figure 2.1.)

By collaboratively completing priority standard summary charts and using them to guide instruction, teachers ensured that all students would be working toward the same *I can* statements (priority standards or targets written in student-friendly terms), all students would be held to the same levels of proficiency, and all students would be exposed to background vocabulary and prerequisite skills.

Summary Chart	
Subject area: _____	Grade: _____
Priority standard (standard number and description):	Planning: • When will we teach this standard (window of days or weeks with dates)?
Unwrapped targets:	• What common assessments will we use to measure student mastery (pretests, formative assessments, and summative assessments)?
I can statement or standard description (in student-friendly words):	• What intervention strategies could we use for students having difficulty mastering the priority standard?
Level of rigor (depth of knowledge) with a proficiency example for each target:	• What enrichment strategies could we use for students who have already mastered the power standard?
Prerequisite skills or vocabulary:	

Source: Thomas, 2015. Reprinted with permission.

Figure 2.1: Standards summary chart.

*Visit **go.SolutionTree.com/PLCbooks** for a free reproducible version of this figure.*

When teachers left for the summer that school year, they knew they wouldn't be gone for long. The vast majority of teachers participated in multiple professional learning and curriculum development sessions over the summer months to prepare for the upcoming school year with a new plan and renewed hope. Because the district did not have a guaranteed and viable reading curriculum, East Detroit adopted state-created reading instructional units. Grade-level curriculum teams spent the summer pouring over the content, adjusting the pacing, identifying the essential standards, and creating both the common summative and common formative assessments that it would use in the coming year. It was a summer of true collaboration for teachers.

The toughest work, however, would come in the fall. Not only were these teachers implementing new units of instruction and new assessments, they were being asked to use a completely foreign style of instruction. The newly adopted reading units used a reading workshop model, which was unfamiliar to most of the staff, who were accustomed to a one-size-fits-all model of reading instruction and now were expected to implement both reading workshop and guided-reading practices. However, East Detroit administrators and the intermediate school district were committed to supporting the teachers. The Macomb Intermediate School District provided coaches to help teachers implement the new practices and provide moral encouragement and support. The district expected principals to be instructional leaders who spent a large amount of time in classrooms offering feedback. And the intermediate school district consultant supported the curriculum director, building principals, coaches, and teachers. These were big changes and, for most, it was an extremely difficult transition.

Teacher teams continued to meet weekly before school, only now they were beginning to review the data derived from common formative and summative assessments. The district created protocols for meetings, for analyzing data, and for providing the principal with feedback at the end of the meetings. All the pieces were in place. However, it was easy to see that team meetings with the principal present were much different than those for which the principal was not present. When the principal was present, teachers were more likely to engage in deeper discussions and ask questions to help clarify the team's thinking. But once the principal left, the tone changed and the meeting often returned to a focus on completing forms or calculating data. Teams were not having enough discussions on their own about the meaning of data or the instructional strategies members used to obtain their results. Even more surprising (or maybe disheartening), was the fact that, despite having data that showed that a significant number of students did not master the target, teachers would rarely plan a specific intervention to help those students. They might say that they would revisit that target with the students who were struggling, but very rarely did they design and deliver the help students really needed. Teachers weren't purposely ignoring these students; they simply did not know what to do next. They needed to learn how to operate as an effective collaborative team within a PLC.

We know that successfully leading a PLC is more about asking questions than giving answers. As Cassandra Erkens and Eric Twadell (2012) state, "Leaders in this context cannot be givers of answers; instead, they frame the important questions, call the appropriate stakeholders to the table, set the guidelines for the conversation, and then engage the system in finding its own right answers" (p. 19). When principals, coaches, or the intermediate school district consultant attended collaborative team meetings, they instinctively asked questions to help the teams go deeper in their discussions.

For example, when teachers in one team noticed that most students got item nine wrong on a test, the teachers automatically assumed it was a bad test question that they should throw out. However, coaches asked the team to look more closely at the test item. They encouraged teachers to ask themselves the following questions.

- "Was there vocabulary in the item that students may have misunderstood?"
- "Did we adequately teach that vocabulary?"
- "Would that vocabulary also be present on state exams for this grade level?"

They also asked team members to go back and examine the students' answers, asking questions like:

- "Did most students get the same wrong answer?"
- "What themes exist among the wrong answers?"
- "What do those themes say about our instructional strategies?"

This type of questioning, which will vary in content with each individual team's needs, helped teams maintain their focus on the four critical questions of a PLC. However, principals and coaches could not attend every teacher team meeting to help teams focus on the right work. The district needed a mechanism to help empower teams to ask these questions themselves. Thus, the pathway tools were created. (This document was originally titled PLC Meeting Guidance, and it appears in chapter 5 on pages 88–89.)

The pathways tool guides teams through a series of probing questions related to the work of PLCs. Teams identify the focus for the meeting and locate the corresponding pathway. For example, if teachers are beginning to plan a new unit, the team may agree to follow the unit-planning pathway, which asks questions about the targets of instruction, which strategies the team will use, and which common formative assessments to deliver. If the team is at the point of analyzing common assessment data, it follows that pathway, which asks questions about proficiency rates for specific targets and how teams will intervene for students who did not show mastery. The East Detroit teams that used the pathways reported that the tool helped them maintain their focus on the critical questions of a PLC. Laurie Hillebrand, a classroom teacher during this process and now a principal in the same school, states that the pathways "provided the foundation each group needed to stay on task and make the most of our time during meetings" (L. Hillebrand, personal communication, November 23, 2015). The principals, coaches, and other observers of team meetings noted a marked difference in the tone of meetings and teachers' engagement levels as they operated within the teams. There was also a noticeable improvement in student achievement data.

The many changes taking place in the East Detroit Public Schools began to have a positive result on students. Scores on the Northwest Evaluation Association (NWEA) assessment rose significantly in these schools consistently in the years following the implementation of PLCs, including the delivery of a guaranteed and viable curriculum, and the addition of instructional coaches who also used the pathways to help guide collaborative team meetings (East Detroit Public Schools, n.d.). For example, in the fall of 2016, nine out of eleven grade levels (82 percent) ranked above the fiftieth percentile nationally for the fall-to-fall NWEA Reading School Conditional Growth Percentile compared to three out of eleven grade levels (27 percent) in fall 2014. Additionally, there was an 82 percentage–point increase in the number of grades with 50 percent or more of students who met or exceeded their RIT growth projections for the fall-to-fall NWEA Reading from fall 2014 to fall 2016. Of course, there are multiple initiatives that led to East Detroit's increases in student scores, and these schools still have a long way to go toward achieving high levels of learning for all students. There is no doubt, however, that PLC transformation plays a significant part in these improvements.

It is important to note, however, that there is a danger in using a tool like the pathways, wherein it becomes just another checklist. When coaches use the pathways as a general guide that leads to deeper questioning, the team is more likely to avoid the checklist mentality. The combination of a coach and a tool (such as the pathways) provides a school with common expectations for collaborative teams and can help hold teachers accountable for their development as a team, and their development as effective instructors. Most important, it can help both coaches and teacher teams use their time wisely by maintaining their focus on instructional practices and student learning.

Conclusion

In this chapter we have discussed how coaches can help schools live the three big ideas of a PLC by building a collaborative culture, maintaining a focus on learning, and sustaining a results orientation. We have also explored ways in which coaches can assist collaborative teams in responding to the four critical questions of a PLC. Finally, we introduced the pathways for supporting teams in the PLC process through a case study of the East Detroit Public Schools. In part II, we will look deeper into the coaching framework by examining the elements of clarity, feedback, and support.

PART II

THE FRAMEWORK FOR COACHING COLLABORATIVE TEAMS

CHAPTER 3

Amplifying Your Impact With Clarity

The importance of clarity is based on the premises that we move toward what is clearest to us and that it is very difficult to create what we cannot describe in detail.

—NICHOLAS SPARKS

When reflecting on the growth and popularity of the PLC process as a model of school improvement, DuFour and colleagues (2016) comment:

> It has been interesting to observe the growing popularity of the term *professional learning community*. In fact, the term has become so commonplace and has been used so ambiguously to describe virtually any loose coupling of individuals who share a common interest in education that it is in danger of losing all meaning. (p. 10)

They go on to point out that, "This lack of precision is an obstacle to implementing PLC processes" (p. 10).

Indeed, clarity is key. This clarity is a fundamental element of our coaching framework. Before teachers can benefit from collaboration's power, they must understand what it takes to fully implement the PLC process. As we mention in the introduction to this book, a critical difference between teams operating as either PLC lite or PLC right is a thorough understanding of the PLC process. Districts and schools can create greater clarity by involving the faculty and staff in the development of a strategy implementation guide that describes the specific behaviors associated with the PLC process.

For some, development of the SIG might occur at a district level and reflect input from district, school, and teacher leaders. For others, the SIG may be developed at a school level where the process includes a representative cross-section of stakeholders. Both scenarios are effective because the process of creating a SIG is the same even if the participants are not.

Engaging the faculty and staff in the process of developing a SIG promotes clarity, builds shared knowledge, creates ownership, and encourages the development of a common vocabulary. It also establishes a standard of best PLC practice and allows teams to measure their progress toward becoming high-performing collaborative teams.

The synergy team members create when collaborating is positive, palpable, and recognizable. In this chapter, we describe a collaborative process coaches can use to amplify the impact coaching has on high-performing teams in a PLC: the development and implementation of a SIG. We describe a SIG, identify the reasons it is useful, give background on the original SIG, go over its content, and describe the process of creating and field-testing this tool.

The Strategy Implementation Guide

Our approach to coaching collaborative teams begins with the development of a SIG that, when fully implemented, reduces variance in team practice, builds shared knowledge, promotes common goals, and supports collaboration as teacher relationships shift from independence to interdependence. Building the capacity of teams to improve student learning is the overarching goal of coaching collaborative teams.

The SIG is the basis for increasing clarity around a team's PLC practices. Teams all begin the PLC process at different levels and mature at different rates. Coaching with the SIG optimizes cycles of continuous improvement and guides coaches and teams as they determine current reality, identify next steps, create short- and long-term goals, and write action plans. The SIG helps monitor the development of PLC practices and provides coaches with a road map for improving the performance of collaborative teams.

This tool can also be called a continuum or rubric. Some schools use rubrics for evaluative purposes while continuums represent resources that guide the curriculum's development. To be as precise as possible, we chose the term *strategy implementation guide* to describe the tool we use to help teams improve their PLC practices.

- *Strategy* acknowledges that PLC is our choice for an overarching school-improvement plan of action.

- *Implementation* describes the process coaches and teams engage in to create the conditions for high-performing collaborative teams.

- *Guide* conveys how coaches will use the document to provide feedback to teams.

Regardless of whether your school calls it a *continuum*, a *rubric*, or a *SIG*, it is important to decide on the terminology you will use when developing the tool that coaches will use to guide the development of collaborative teams.

When the faculty and staff create a SIG to describe an effective PLC, they amplify the clarity teams have around their practice. Based on our experience, school and district leaders who have led their staff in creating a SIG report that the process was one of the most positive professional development opportunities their teams experienced.

Reason for the SIG

The coaching process is more efficient and effective when coaches have an objective point of reference (such as a continuum, rubric, or SIG) that describes the progression teachers follow as they move from initial practice to full integration of new skills in their classroom. According to coaching expert Bruce Wellman (2009), "By establishing a third point of reference with both exemplars and examples of the teachers' own results, the conversation becomes one of analysis and objective evaluation about the results not a judgment of the person" (p. 7).

John Hattie (2015c) urges educators to focus on reducing the variability between classrooms as a way to improve teaching and learning. Using a SIG to coach teams around improving their PLC practices promotes the development of a common language, which contributes to greater clarity. As clarity increases and a team's understanding of important PLC concepts grows, the amount of variability among and between collaborative teams decreases.

Previously we made the point that clarity is critical to improving collaborative teams, but sometimes schools ask coaches to intervene without a deep understanding of what the next steps for the team might be. The SIG provides coaches with an agreed-on standard of best PLC practice, and, when using a SIG, they can readily identify areas of potential improvement and provide the kind of support teams need to become high-performing collaborative teams.

A SIG promotes consistent monitoring of collaborative teams. By identifying the next steps teams should consider, coaches, principals, and teachers themselves are able to track the development of PLC practices in their schools. Progress monitoring connected to specific descriptors allows feedback to flow, differentiated coaching to occur, and meaningful goal-setting to take place. These job-embedded professional development opportunities provide powerful just-in-time learning for collaborative teams.

Using a SIG also promotes continuous improvement. Feedback is more consistent, and conversations between the coach and the team benefit from suggestions designed to help teams move from one level of the SIG to the next. It is an excellent way to celebrate growth as teams continue to improve.

In spite of what we know, some leaders choose to direct the development of PLCs by tightly prescribing specific steps teams must take to achieve the desired outcomes. This top-down, too-tight approach creates compliance, but our goal is to generate a high level of commitment (DuFour et al., 2016). Engaging staff in the creation of a SIG increases ownership and helps schools meet that goal.

The most effective coaches and school leaders know the best way to build ownership is to involve the faculty in the process of defining outcomes together. We also know that asking teachers to participate in the development process takes more time, but in the end, the results are worth it. Engaging teachers in the process of building a SIG creates a deeper commitment to improving the PLC process.

Some districts begin with coaches, principals, and teacher leaders creating the first draft of a SIG and then involving teachers during the revision phase. Other districts begin the initial draft of a SIG at the building level, working with grade-level or subject-specific teams. District-level implementation requires that, at some point, team members or leaders from different buildings will meet to reconcile the various SIGs into a common SIG the district can use. We find that either way the process unfolds, it creates more clarity at all levels of the system when the various stakeholders are involved in creating a SIG.

Several excellent PLC continua that teams can use as the basis of their own SIG already exist; some of the best appear in *Learning by Doing: A Handbook for Professional Learning Communities at Work, Third Edition.* Among our favorites are Clarifying What Students Must Learn (DuFour et al., 2016, pp. 128–129) and Providing Students With Systematic Interventions and Extensions (DuFour et al., 2016, pp. 176–177).

The continua in *Learning by Doing* provide a solid foundation and represent a great entry point for districts and schools as they start the process of developing their own SIG. In the PLC process, the first critical question—What do we want students to know and be able to do?—requires that collaborative teams engage in deep dialogue around national and state standards to understand and prioritize essentials outcomes. Because teams are examining standards they did not write themselves, the value of prioritizing comes from the dialogue team members have as they make meaning and reach consensus on what their students must learn and be able to do.

This process is similar to the way districts, schools, and teams begin to develop their own SIG. Teams we have worked with start with dialogue around existing continuums like those in *Learning by Doing* (DuFour et al., 2016). They take their learning to another level by unwrapping the components of the PLC process, identifying specific behaviors and actionable steps, and creating their own SIG to guide themselves to higher levels of implementation.

We acknowledge the temptation to use an existing continuum as the foundation for coaching teams to save time and energy, but there is a cost for taking this shortcut. When teachers are part of developing a SIG, they simultaneously deepen their understanding and build ownership of the outcomes they seek to achieve. Again, designing a SIG collaboratively results in a much deeper understanding of the PLC process and a much stronger commitment to improving a team's PLC practices.

A well-constructed SIG increases clarity by providing a well-defined set of descriptions for teams to use when implementing each element of the PLC process. It provides teams with the criteria for assessing their current level of development, tracking their progress, and identifying the next steps they must take to reach a proficient level of performance on each element of the PLC process. Finally, the SIG establishes the standards of best PLC practice that anchor the process of providing feedback that we will discuss in chapter 4 (page 67).

Practitioner Perspective

Understanding and making sense of our SIG was an exciting endeavor for our school. We had many schoolwide discussions to come to a common understanding of the SIG and how to make it our own. We self-assessed our teams and made goals for where we wanted to head next. These goals then helped guide our professional learning. We knew we had to continue to move forward in order to fulfill our promise to our students. In the end, we had a working tool that we will continue to revise over time. But, regardless, it is a beginning point that serves as the launching point for our collective work.

—**ALAINA SEERY**, Kindergarten Teacher, Jeffco Public Schools, Jefferson County, Colorado (personal communication, January 18, 2017)

Transparency about a SIG's intent and purpose is important. A SIG is *not* a tool to rank the teams' effectiveness or for use in any evaluative process; we argue against using a SIG for evaluation of any kind. The formation of high-performing collaborative teams is predicated on an inquiry model that encourages continuous improvement, risk taking, and midcourse corrections. The SIG is a developmental tool that supports teacher teams, coaches, and school leaders in articulating a team's current reality, identifying implementation gaps, and designing next steps. As Joellen Killion (2015) states, teacher teams will engage, improve, self-direct, and take pride in their performance when they have time to comprehend what's expected of them, understand what their goals are, know how well they're achieving those goals, and have time to self-correct.

> ### Practitioner Perspective
>
> Our school looked to our SIG to ground us in our core PLC beliefs. As we began using it in all collaborative team meetings, it helped us recognize the importance and how all the elements of the PLC coaching cycle intertwined. We also held a mindset that a continuum is constantly in draft form and, as we learned more about how effective collaborative teams operate, it should be refined.
>
> **—SHARON IVIE**, Principal, Jeffco Schools, Jefferson County, Colorado (personal communication, May 4, 2016)

The Original SIG

The SIG we present in this book is based on an original SIG designed by Lisa Guzzardo Asaro of the Macomb County Integrated School District (ISD), Macomb County, Michigan, and Ben Boerkoel, Kent ISD school improvement consultant, in 2012. Asaro and Dodie McGuire Raycraft of the Macomb County ISD further refined the document in 2014. As the primary author, Asaro explains the original thinking behind the creation and use of a SIG:

> In our work as school improvement consultants for two large counties in Michigan, we found that, even though schools and districts identified research-based strategies in their continuous improvement plans, they frequently failed to achieve the targets identified by their measureable goals. Upon further investigation, it became clear that, in many cases, those implementing the strategies had a variety of interpretations of what fidelity looked and sounded like; thereby also making it difficult to monitor implementation and provide feedback. Based on our own observation of practice as well as field testing by our colleagues through the Michigan Department of Education's Michigan Continuous School Improvement (MI-CSI) Task Force, it is our belief that having users create and implement a Strategy Implementation Guide (SIG) is critical to implementation with fidelity.
>
> Our SIG was grounded in a common understanding of the critical components of each strategy (non-negotiables) based on research. It also used research to identify the "gold standard" of implementation of each component, possible acceptable variations that will still bring the expected results, and unacceptable variations that will not bring those same results. (L. Asaro, personal communication, October 22, 2017)

Asaro summarizes the best way to use a SIG:

> The power of a SIG is not only in its initial creation and agreed-on components, but also in its use for reflection. It can be used individually for self-reflection, in conversations in PLC teams, and in conversations with coaches. The intent is that it *not* be used for evaluation; rather, it should be used as a means for providing feedback to increase the quality of instruction. (L. Asaro, personal communication, October 22, 2017)

With permission, we have adapted the work of Asaro, Boerkoel, and Raycraft as the basis for the SIG for PLCs that we present in this book.

Content of the SIG

Effective coaches and leaders recognize the importance of articulating the parameters and expectations around a PLC's essential elements. Teams thrive on the autonomy to make decisions within clearly defined limits; this is the essence of loose-tight leadership (DuFour et al., 2016; Sagie, 1997).

In PLC schools across the United States, collaborative teams operate in unique ways and develop the systems and structures that work best for them. There are often differences in the specific ways that teams operate, but what they all have in common is a focus on the outcomes associated with each essential element of a PLC—the three big ideas and four critical questions—as defined by Richard DuFour and his colleagues (DuFour et al., 2016).

In his keynote presentation "In Praise of American Educators . . . And How They Can Get Even Better," Richard DuFour (2015) concisely articulated five prerequisites that are essential when establishing a PLC.

1. Educators work in collaborative teams and take collective responsibility for student learning rather than working in isolation.

2. Collaborative teams implement a guaranteed and viable curriculum, unit by unit.

3. Collaborative teams monitor student learning through an ongoing assessment process that includes frequent, team-developed common formative assessments.

4. Educators use the results of common assessments to improve individual practice, build the team's capacity to achieve its goals, and intervene and enrich on behalf of students.

5. The school provides a systematic process for intervention and enrichment.

We advocate that at a *minimum*, a SIG must align to these five items; more specifically, a team's policies, practices, and procedures must align to these elements of the PLC process.

The Process of Creating a SIG

As we mentioned earlier in the chapter, creation of a SIG can be a district-level or school-level endeavor. In our experience, engaging different stakeholders from different levels of the school system provides an excellent opportunity for participants to make meaning of their practice; the very act of drafting and designing a SIG is an opportunity for some outstanding professional development.

What a district and individual schools include in their SIGs may vary somewhat. Different levels of the school system may emphasize different elements of the PLC process, highlighting different priorities by what team members choose to include on a SIG, and identifying different approaches to improving practice. If there are differences, however, it is vital that the SIGs are eventually aligned from the team to the school to the district level. The number of people who help craft a SIG can also vary from level to level. We highly recommend that multiple stakeholders be involved in the process at all levels.

Creating a SIG at the district level should involve district leaders, school (building) leaders, coaches, and a representative sample of teachers from across the district. Creating a SIG at the school level should involve district leaders, school (building) leaders, coaches, and members of the building's teacher leadership team.

While the contents of a SIG may differ from level to level, the basic structure of a SIG remains the same regardless of whether it is designed to be used at the district or school level. The same is true regardless of the stakeholders involved in its creation—the process of creating a SIG remains the same.

The process of creating a SIG is collaborative, so teams must have time set aside that is devoted to this work. While it is good to capitalize on teachers' enthusiasm early on in any team endeavor, the beginning stages of SIG development require patience. Indeed, educators have a well-earned reputation for wanting to fully implement an idea "by the end of the day tomorrow." Those drafting the SIG should realize that their initial document will have strengths to build on and weaknesses too address. No matter how well written the SIG, it requires review and revision. Communicating this information to the faculty and staff prior to their work helps instill a mindset that the SIG will always be evolving.

A SIG consists of a series of anchor statements and a matching progression of indicators describing different levels of implementation for each PLC element the SIG highlights. The following sections highlight the steps a team takes in creating a SIG.

Step 1: Identify Elements of the PLC Process

The first step in creating a SIG is to reach consensus on the elements of the PLC process that teams will monitor at the district or school level. We recommend that, at a minimum, a SIG include DuFour's (2015) five prerequisite conditions for establishing a PLC (see pages 53–54). These agreements reflect what is tight or nondiscretionary in a PLC.

Step 2: Write Anchor Statements

Step 2 is to write anchor statements. An anchor statement creates a vivid description of fully successful performance of each prerequisite condition of a PLC. Based on what is known about an effective PLC, participants define what a school or district's practice would look like, feel like, and sound like when the corresponding anchor statement is fully implemented at the highest level. Once the team has reached consensus on the descriptions of best practice, these anchor statements go into the farthest left column of the SIG, as in the example in figure 3.1.

Anchor Statements	Beyond Proficient	Proficient	Below Proficient
Educators work in collaborative teams and take collective responsibilities for student learning rather than working in isolation.			
Collaborative teams implement a guaranteed and viable curriculum, unit by unit.			
Collaborative teams monitor student learning through an ongoing assessment process that includes frequent, team-developed, common formative assessments.			

Figure 3.1: Anchor statements in a SIG.

continued →

Anchor Statements	Beyond Proficient	Proficient	Below Proficient
Educators use the results of common assessments to improve individual practice, build the team's capacity to achieve its goals, and intervene and enrich on behalf of students.			
The school provides a systematic process for intervention and enrichment.			

Step 3: Develop Indicators

The third step is to create a set of indicators for each anchor statement. An *indicator* describes the level of implementation a district or school would need to achieve to be considered below, meeting, or exceeding levels of proficiency. Indicators are developmental, describing a progression and defining a trajectory toward the condition the anchor statement describes.

When drafting each set of indicators (below proficient, proficient, and beyond proficient), participants consider such things as what actions are necessary to move from one indicator to the next; what resources will teams need, who will provide them, and how they will be delivered; and who will be responsible for providing clarity, feedback, and support for the teams. The best place to begin thinking about the indicators is with the middle category describing what constitutes proficient performance for the corresponding anchor statement.

Some variation to what is defined as best practice in a PLC is acceptable at the proficient level, but those variations may not impede a district or school's progress toward achieving the level of implementation the anchor statement describes. Proficient levels of implementation suggest that while existing levels of PLC practice may not be fully developed, the current practice does not compromise or alter the overall trajectory of improvement efforts. Once a team has reached consensus, members inserts the language describing what proficiency looks like into the middle indicator column of the SIG (see figure 3.2).

For those implementing at a beyond proficient level, little or no variation exists between the PLC practice in the anchor statement and current practice in the district or at the school. Once the team has drafted a description of what beyond proficient implementation looks like, it gets inserted into the left indicator column of the SIG (see figure 3.3, page 58).

Anchor Statements	Beyond Proficient	Proficient	Below Proficient
Educators work in collaborative teams, rather than in isolation, and take collective responsibility for student learning.		Teachers meet weekly in collaborative teams for a minimum of forty-five minutes during the regular school day. They write norms and goals, and participated in common planning to improve student learning.	
Collaborative teams implement a guaranteed and viable curriculum, unit by unit.		Teacher teams prioritize and unwrap standards, identify learning targets, and follow pacing guides created by the district or the publisher.	
Collaborative teams monitor student learning through an ongoing assessment process that includes frequent, team-developed, common formative assessments.		Teacher teams share the responsibility for creating common formative and summative assessments they administer on a regular basis throughout the school year.	
Educators use the results of common assessments to improve individual practice, build the team's capacity to achieve its goals, and intervene and enrich on behalf of students.		Teacher teams analyze the results of common formative and summative assessments to identify which students need more time and support.	
The school provides a systematic process for intervention and enrichment.		Teacher teams provide students with remedial support as well as targeted interventions that are systematic, practical, effective, essential, and directive.	

Figure 3.2: Indicators for proficiency in a SIG.

Anchor Statements	Beyond Proficient	Proficient	Below Proficient
Educators work in collaborative teams, rather than in isolation, and take collective responsibility for student learning.	Teachers meet weekly in collaborative teams for a minimum of sixty minutes during the regular school day. They utilize norms, goals, and protocols and work interdependently to improve their practice and enhance student learning.	Teachers meet weekly in collaborative teams for a minimum of forty-five minutes during the regular school day. They write norms and goals, and participated in common planning to improve student learning.	
Collaborative teams implement a guaranteed and viable curriculum, unit by unit.	Teams prioritize and unwrap standards, identify learning targets, write *I can* statements, create common pacing guides, and commit to teach—rather than cover—the curriculum.	Teacher teams prioritize and unwrap standards, identify learning targets, and follow pacing guides created by the district or the publisher.	
Collaborative teams monitor student learning through an ongoing assessment process that includes frequent, team-developed, common formative assessments.	Teacher teams work collaboratively to create valid and reliable common formative and summative assessments they administer every few weeks throughout the school year.	Teacher teams share the responsibility for creating common formative and summative assessments they administer on a regular basis throughout the school year.	
Educators use the results of common assessments to improve individual practice, build the team's capacity to achieve its goals, and intervene and enrich on behalf of students.	Teacher teams analyze common formative and summative assessment results to identify which students need more time and support and which instructional strategies they should retain, refine, or replace.	Teacher teams analyze the results of common formative and summative assessments to identify which students need more time and support.	
The school provides a systematic process for intervention and enrichment.	Teacher teams provide students with enrichment and remedial support as well as targeted and timely interventions that are systematic, practical, effective, essential, and directive, without missing direct instruction in another core subject.	Teacher teams provide students with remedial support as well as targeted interventions that are systematic, practical, effective, essential, and directive.	

Figure 3.3: Indicators for beyond proficiency in a SIG.

Finally, the indicator for the below-proficient category describes conditions that, if not addressed, will negatively impact the successful implementation of the PLC process. These descriptions are inserted into the right indicator column of the SIG (see figure 3.4).

Anchor Statements	Beyond Proficient	Proficient	Below Proficient
Educators work in collaborative teams, rather than in isolation, and take collective responsibility for student learning.	Teachers meet weekly in collaborative teams for a minimum of sixty minutes during the regular school day. They utilize norms, goals, and protocols and work interdependently to improve their practice and enhance student learning.	Teachers meet weekly in collaborative teams for a minimum of forty-five minutes during the regular school day. They write norms and goals, and participated in common planning to improve student learning.	Teachers meet weekly in collaborative teams for a minimum of forty-five minutes per week outside the regular school day. They work together on topics of mutual interest and share ideas, materials, and resources.
Collaborative teams implement a guaranteed and viable curriculum, unit by unit.	Teams prioritize and unwrap standards, identify learning targets, write *I can* statements, create common pacing guides, and commit to teach—rather than cover—the curriculum.	Teacher teams prioritize and unwrap standards, identify learning targets, and follow pacing guides created by the district or the publisher.	Teachers deliver lessons based on what they know the best, like the most, have materials for, or what is included in the textbooks.
Collaborative teams monitor student learning through an ongoing assessment process that includes frequent, team-developed, common formative assessments.	Teacher teams work collaboratively to create valid and reliable common formative and summative assessments they administer every few weeks throughout the school year.	Teacher teams share the responsibility for creating common formative and summative assessments they administer on a regular basis throughout the school year.	Teacher teams rotate the responsibility for creating common summative assessments they administer periodically throughout the school year.
Educators use the results of common assessments to improve individual practice, build the team's capacity to achieve its goals, and intervene and enrich on behalf of students.	Teacher teams analyze common formative and summative assessment results to identify which students need more time and support and which instructional strategies they should retain, refine, or replace.	Teacher teams analyze the results of common formative and summative assessments to identify which students need more time and support.	Teacher teams review summative assessment results to monitor student progress or generate grades.

Figure 3.4: Anchor statements in a SIG.

continued →

Anchor Statements	Beyond Proficient	Proficient	Below Proficient
The school provides a systematic process for intervention and enrichment.	Teacher teams provide students with enrichment and remedial support as well as targeted and timely interventions that are systematic, practical, effective, essential, and directive, without missing direct instruction in another core subject.	Teacher teams provide students with remedial support as well as targeted interventions that are systematic, practical, effective, essential, and directive.	Teacher teams provide students with opportunities to receive additional remedial support.

Visit **go.SolutionTree.com/PLCbooks** to find other examples of SIGs.

Practitioner Perspective

Our team has used our SIG for our own self-assessment. We looked to it for a way to begin a whole-group conversation about our progress as a collaborative team. We didn't tackle all the elements or indicators at the beginning. Instead, we focused our conversations at the start. By having the individual descriptors that mapped out progressions, the continuum helped us reflect and refine our PLC practices. In the end, we were proud of the progress we made over time. I do believe having access to the continuum [SIG] and input into creating it was critical to our overall investment in the process.

—**KERRY O'SULLIVAN**, Fifth-Grade Teacher, Jeffco Schools, Jefferson County, Colorado (personal communication, February 18, 2016)

When setting out to create a SIG, members of the faculty and staff participating in the work bring any resources (such as samples, examples, or exemplars of PLC rubrics, continuums, or SIGs) to use as guides. Visit **go.SolutionTree/PLCbooks** to find several examples.

For a principal or district-level leader, the SIG serves as a tool to track the development of PLC practices on a team, at a school, or in the district. District administrators can use a SIG at a macro level to identify consistent patterns or trends in a school or district's overall levels of PLC implementation. Likewise, a principal can engage the school's guiding coalition in conversations based on anchor statements and indicators on the SIG and use that information to support the development of staff and monitor teams' progress. Coaches and team leaders find value in the way a SIG clarifies and defines the desired outcomes of collaborative work. Coaches can use a SIG as a tool to engage teams in reflective dialogue. Ultimately, the most effective reflective conversations are rooted in evidence collected during collaborative team meetings and linked to the specific anchors and indicators on the SIG.

> ### Practitioner Perspective
>
> Our school's SIG has set our standard for PLC implementation. We knew going into it that our understanding of how to create one wasn't perfect. In fact, we had huge doubts we were even close to "getting it right." We framed our ongoing connections as a "work in progress" and this language was important because it reminded everyone that we were learning and implementing together. Over time, we have adjusted our SIG, and that has helped us own the components of our PLC implementation at a deeper level. However, as a principal, I have appreciated the common language and focus it has provided for my staff and me. I feel it has helped teams get on the same page and working toward a common goal. This feels good!
>
> —**NATALIE BERGES TUCKER**, Principal, Jeffco Schools, Jefferson County, Colorado (personal communication, September 30, 2016)

The SIG's Field Test

Software companies recognize the need to build beta testing into their development process. Opportunities to test their products allow designers to identify bugs and glitches that may prevent their software from performing at optimal levels. These beta tests are done on a small scale with end users who have been informed about the nature of the testing.

Developers create feedback loops where users report problems—what did not work or times when the software did not perform as anticipated. Based on the feedback, the engineers make the necessary revisions to improve the product. For companies like Apple, with all their research and development resources, beta testing is a common practice (Apple, 2017). Even after the process of beta testing concludes, there is an ongoing need for continual updates. This kind of recursive process produces a stronger product over time.

Schools and districts can do the same thing with their SIGs. It is hard to resist the urge in the beginning stage, especially for those at the district or central-office level, to simply *fix it*; however, engaging the faculty and staff in developing the SIG creates more ownership and a deeper understanding of the expectations for implementing the PLC process. Let's take a look at a few examples of school systems that successfully created and field-tested a SIG.

In Jefferson County, Colorado, a large district of 154 schools, district and school leadership teams attended multiple professional development sessions devoted to the building of shared knowledge around the three big ideas, four critical questions, and essential elements of a PLC. Implementation of small increments of the PLC process began at each school. Initially the schools experienced both success and missteps as the collaborative teams learned by doing.

After six months of initial implementation, a cadre of district and school leaders, coaches, and teachers met for two days to create an initial draft of a SIG with the intention to create a tool to guide districtwide implementation of PLCs. They titled their SIG the Jeffco PLC Implementation Continuum. (See **go.SolutionTree.com /PLCbooks** to access the SIG online.)

Once a draft of Jeffco's SIG was completed, the development team met for one additional day to field-test their version of a SIG. In the morning, these administrative and teacher leaders spread out across the district and simultaneously observed multiple team meetings, in real time, at multiple locations. Administrative and teacher leaders, the same people who had written the initial draft of the SIG, observed collaborative team meetings, took notes, and identified places where the SIG did and did not work.

Later that same day, the teachers, coaches, and principals reconvened into small teams and reached consensus on any adjustments they felt should be made to the initial draft of the SIG. A smaller writing team synthesized the common themes that had emerged from the field-testing and revised the initial draft accordingly.

The small team then sent a second draft of the SIG to school leadership teams for another review. Principals reported that this final step honored the time teachers had invested in field-testing the SIG, allowed for more clarification, and provided closure to the development process. When school leaders who field-tested the SIG reflected on the experience, they found that the most important outcomes of the field-testing were the opportunity for systemwide calibration of the anchor statements and indicators on the SIG and a deepening of the teachers' collective understanding of best PLC practices.

In East Detroit Public Schools, a much smaller school system consisting of four schools began implementing PLCs in a similar way. District, school, coaches, and teacher leaders participated in common PLC training that coincided with initial efforts to implement the PLC process at the school sites.

After a period of training and initial implementation, the same group who had participated in the initial round of professional development met for one day to create a draft of their own strategy implementation guide. When the draft was completed, the leadership team from East Detroit used the same process Jeffco Schools had used to test their SIG.

Rather than observing teams in real time and at multiple locations, each East Detroit principal brought a video of a team meeting to a training session with others who had designed the original SIG. Principals, teachers, coaches, and district-level staff imagined themselves in the role of coach as they reviewed the contents of the SIG, watched the recorded team meetings, analyzed the PLC practices, and role played delivering the kind of feedback that would move a team from its current to next levels of collaboration as described in the SIG.

Using recorded team meetings has several advantages over observing teams in real time. First, it is more flexible, easier to schedule, and can be replicated. Second, this process gave the district's teacher leaders and administrators an opportunity to develop a higher level of inter-rater reliability while simultaneously calibrating their understanding of the indicators on the district's SIG. Third, it reinforced common language and built shared knowledge of best PLC practices. Finally, as leaders worked and learned together, they developed a greater sense of efficacy around the district's ability to monitor the development of the PLC process. After this meeting, leaders created a subcommittee to revise the SIG based on comments and observations made during the training, similar to the process utilized in Jefferson Schools.

As you consider the benefits of creating a strategy implementation guide, remember that in the end, collaboratively creating and field-testing the SIG creates great clarity around what it takes to successfully implement the PLC process. See figure 3.5 (pages 64–65) for a sample SIG.

Practitioner Perspective

As an instructional coach, I find that our SIG has been instrumental to my work with teacher teams. I access it all the time! I use it to provide feedback, monitor progress, set goals, and push teams to greater implementation. Using the continuum has increased my skills as a coach. It has given me the focus to coach teacher teams. As a new coach, having the SIG has really helped to guide my work. It has made all the difference for both me and the teachers I work with on a daily basis.

—**SHANNON CARLSON**, Instructional Coach, Jeffco Schools, Jefferson County, Colorado (personal communication, January 17, 2017)

Critical Component How does this component contribute to the overall outcome of this practice?	Gold Standard of Implementation What should the team do to implement the critical component well?	Acceptable Variation of Implementation What adaptations are acceptable without losing value?	Unacceptable Variation of Implementation What defines unacceptable implementation?
A balanced, coherent system of common formative assessments based on a viable curriculum is in place.	• The team clarifies or adjusts essential outcomes by grade or course as necessary. • The team establishes targets and benchmarks. • The team develops common assessments. • The team analyzes assessment results. • The team plans for interventions and instructional improvement strategies.	• Team members can use previous common assessments with necessary modifications.	• Team members can use assessments in isolation or use those that are not common to a grade level, course, or subject area.
Review of the student data will be possible.	• Team members arrive having reviewed individual data and are ready to plan assessments or instruction. • Team members bring data to the meeting in the predetermined, usable format. • The team reviews group data using a previously agreed-on protocol. • The team analyzes assessment results.	• Team members review individual classroom data for five minutes at the beginning of the meeting. • The team decides on the protocol on the spot. • The individual data is present but in varied formats.	• Team members do not review individual data before the meeting, and this becomes the meeting's focus. • Data review takes longer than ten minutes. • The team has no protocol for reviewing data as a team. • The individual data does not represent the desired outcomes of the meeting.

| The team uses student data to plan instruction, assessment, and intervention or enrichment. | • The team publicly discusses these data to inform instruction and to promote high levels of learning for all students.

• The team arrives with a diverse toolbox of strategies and resources to address needs the data set identifies.

• Team planning draws from the instructional learning cycle and is consistent from classroom to classroom. Variations may occur within student grouping and subject areas based on the data set.

• The team analyzes data to design remediation, interventions, and enrichments to meet the instructional needs of all students.

• The team analyzes data to identify which instructional practices members need to retain, revise, or replace. | • The team is prepared to apply strategies once members completely review the data.

• The team uses limited best practices in planning.

• Planning is fairly consistent from classroom to classroom. | • The team does not use data in planning.

• Planning is inconsistent from classroom to classroom.

• Assessments are not consistent from classroom to classroom within a building. |

Source: © 2017; Adapted from Van Dyke Public Schools, Warren, Michigan.

Figure 3.5: Sample completed SIG.

*Visit **go.SolutionTree.com/PLCbooks** for a free reproducible version of this figure.*

A Cycle of Continuous Improvement

When districts or schools create a SIG, they get crystal clear on the conditions necessary for implementing the PLC process. District administrators, coaches, principals, and teachers begin to utilize the SIG as the source of data for ongoing cycles of continuous improvement.

Collecting objective data connected to anchor statements and indicators within the SIG becomes common practice. Coaches help teams confront the hard facts around gaps in implementation while keeping focused on opportunities for incremental improvement. Coaches' subjective opinions are replaced by objective feedback based on the anchors and indicators built into the SIG. Gaps in practice become easier to pinpoint and prioritize. The natural progression of PLC practice defined within the SIG empowers coaches and teams to come together to cocreate purposeful action plans that supports development of the PLC process.

Conclusion

When coaches work with teacher teams and principals to collaborate on the creation of a SIG, the SIG becomes a versatile tool that all stakeholders can use as the basis of improvement efforts. For individuals coaching collaborative teams, the SIG serves as a guide that defines the collective actions team members undertake to improve.

Teams benefit from time to reflect on their work. Allowing for dialogue and discussion about the SIG amplifies clarity, creates a sense of ownership, and allows teachers and coaches to internalize the outcomes connected to each element of the PLC process. The intent is that the SIG becomes a living document that is regularly revisited as collaborative teams internalize the steps necessary to fully implementing the PLC model.

In the next chapter, we focus on the second aspect of our coaching framework: amplifying your impact with feedback.

CHAPTER 4

Amplifying Your Impact With Feedback

Feedback is not just what gets ranked; it's what gets thanked, commented on, and invited back or dropped. Feedback can be formal or informal, direct or implicit; it can be blunt or baroque, totally obvious or so subtle that you're not sure what it is.

—DOUGLAS STONE AND SHEILA HEEN

In the best schools, leaders know not to limit feedback to teachers who are new to the profession or struggling in their classroom. Nor should they reserve feedback for teachers who are in the midst of an evaluation cycle. All teachers benefit from having regular opportunities to seek out and receive feedback from their peers and school leaders.

Collaborative teams also benefit from frequent opportunities for feedback. Indeed, highly effective collaborative teams do not occur by hope or happenstance; they need clarity, feedback, and support. This chapter focuses on the second element in our coaching framework: feedback. It defines feedback, identifies what makes good feedback, looks at how to provide feedback and how to apply feedback, and how feedback connects to the SIG.

In traditional one-on-one coaching models, coaches provide feedback to individual teachers. While this practice of individual feedback should continue, we are advocating for a shift in coaching priorities. If schools reallocate their resources, redefine the scope of the coach's role, and prioritize the coaching of collaborative teams, feedback will amplify the positive impact of teams on teaching and learning.

Defining Feedback

A review of the school-improvement literature yields descriptions of many different feedback models. Grant Wiggins (2012) identifies seven key characteristics of effective feedback: it's (1) goal referenced, (2) tangible and transparent, (3) actionable, (4) user friendly (specific and personalized), (5) timely, (6) ongoing, and (7) consistent. George Knight (2014) highlights three helpful traits of effective feedback. He says it has to be (1) expected, (2) positive, and (3) self-reflective. The Victorian Curriculum and Assessment Authority (2014) describes six attributes of effective feedback. It:

1. Improves learning

2. Starts with learning intentions

3. Is timely

4. Is clear and focuses on improvement strategies

5. Encourages reflection

6. Is more than a grade

It seems there is plenty of support for the value of feedback, but less agreement about exactly what constitutes an effective model. The one element common in all the research is the belief that feedback is *essential* to improving performance.

Our working definition of feedback closely aligns with Douglas Stone and Sheila Heen's (2014) definition. In their book *Thanks for the Feedback*, Harvard Law School lecturers Stone and Heen (2014) define feedback as "any information you get about yourself" (p. 4). They note:

> It [feedback] is how we learn about ourselves from our experiences and from other people—how we learn from life. It's your annual performance review, the firm's climate survey, the local critic's review of your restaurant. But feedback also includes the way your son's eyes light up when he spots you in the audience and the way your friend surreptitiously slips off the sweater you knitted her the minute she thinks you're out of view. It's the speedy renewal of services by a longtime client and the lecture you get from the cop on the side of the road. It's what your bum knee is trying to tell you about your diminishing spryness, and the confusing mix of affection and disdain you get from your fifteen year old. (p. 4)

In short, feedback is how we learn. Killion (2015) suggests that in schools, the word *feedback* can elicit a positive, negative, or neutral response. For those with a negative connotation, their experience with feedback may connect to state or province and federal mandates or conjure up archaic evaluation systems that make judgments about teacher effectiveness. In order to diminish the potential for a negative reaction to feedback, coaches can help teachers understand that feedback is neither positive nor negative; it is best thought as of a mirror that reflects back practice.

Feedback that emanates from the collection of objective data helps paint a picture of actual practice and sets the stage for team coaching. Grounding feedback in data gathered from an agreed-on standard of best practice (the SIG) increases the likelihood teachers will respond to the feedback positively. If teams perceive feedback to be biased or based on opinion, they are less likely to be open to receiving it.

Defining Good Feedback

Certain conditions must be in place to ensure individual teachers and teacher teams benefit from feedback. For example, it is important that teams believe the person delivering the feedback has positive intentions about the team, its work, and the current level of practice; that feedback's purpose is to foster growth and development; and that conversations allow enough time for meaningful reflection both as individuals and teams. Increasing the amount and quality of feedback teams receive may also require a change in the traditional mindset of building principals, coaches, and teachers—especially for those accustomed to traditional instructional coaching models that have a deficit orientation focused on fixing individual teachers (Sweeny, 2011).

Feedback is data based on something that has already happened, so a combination of feedback and coaching is critical; without both, teams stagnate at various stages of PLC implementation. Teams can struggle for a variety of reasons, including a lack of time, focus, or leadership. Using feedback to coach teams creates an environment that supports and promotes cycles of continuous improvement.

Feedback from a coach provides an outside perspective and serves as a catalyst toward improved performance. If effective feedback is present, teams maximize their potential; without it, they are prone to repeating practices that may not be effective. "Practice doesn't make perfect, practice makes permanent" (Lemov, Woolway, & Yazzi, 2012, p. 2), and when ineffective practice becomes the norm, teams plateau or stagnate in their efforts to implement the PLC process.

Coaching enables teams to make sense of and learn from these data so that team members can continue to improve their practices. Providing the right feedback at the right time and in the right context is the key to improvement. Once they share feedback, coaches help teams make the necessary changes to improve their practice.

Table 4.1 provides a list of actions, tools, and resources to help establish the necessary conditions for a feedback-rich environment in schools. You can also find excellent PLC resources on the AllThingsPLC website (www.allthingsplc.info).

Table 4.1: Necessary Conditions for a Feedback-Rich Environment

Actions to Create the Conditions	Tools and Resources to Actualize the Actions
Create awareness and understanding regarding why feedback is important.	Access professional articles, personal stories, and online videos related to growth mindset, feedback, and continuous improvement.
Be transparent about the purpose of feedback and the associated coaching process.	Share information at staff meetings and use multiple means for staff communication, such as one-on-one communication and team time.
Model ways to deliver and receive feedback.	During a staff meeting, role-play examples and nonexamples of feedback conversations. Engage in a fishbowl conversation about how to receive feedback in a productive, action-oriented way. Create a list of important points to remember for when you are either a giver or receiver of feedback.
Ensure transparency regarding the SIG (see chapter 3, page 51). Feedback about PLC implementation is ineffective when the team is unfamiliar with the tool.	Make time to create and embed the SIG as a team-coaching tool with teacher teams. Spend time to ensure new faculty have a common understanding of the vocabulary, terminology, and the process for how feedback connects to the SIG's anchor statements and indicators.

In PLCs, teacher teams commit to build their practice around cycles of continuous improvement (DuFour et al., 2016). These cycles must involve feedback. We argue, however, that feedback alone is not enough. When a school couples frequent feedback with effective coaching, improved levels of productivity for a collaborative team are almost always the result (Shipper, 2009). In our work with countless collaborative teams in PLCs, three themes emerge.

1. In the absence of feedback based on an agreed-on standard, teams will continue to rely on their own perceptions of what effective teaming looks, sounds, and feels like.

2. All teams deserve the opportunity to improve, but without feedback, teams will continue to "do the best they can" given their current level of training and practice.

3. As teams become more collaborative, their perception about feedback shifts from compliance to commitment, from alignment to engagement.

In the end, these themes validate the importance of feedback as a critical component of coaching teams. Belief in the PLC process as a model of continuous improvement is easy to rally around when the energy and excitement of early implementation are present. A team coaching cycle that integrates clarity, feedback, and support maintains that momentum and drives the work forward. Repeatedly, we have witnessed stronger, more effective implementation of the PLC process when teams receive and respond to credible feedback.

Committing to Feedback

In order for feedback to be an effective component of the team coaching process, districts, schools, and teams must commit to ongoing observation and monitoring of teams. The coaching process is predicated on having direct knowledge of a team's current collaborative practice in relation to the SIG. While attending team meetings, coaches use an evidence-based approach to collect objective data over a period of time. Although a brief fifteen-minute observation can provide a coach with useful information about how a team functions, we must remember the importance of seeking a well-rounded view of a team's collaborative processes. It isn't feasible for a coach to attend every team meeting, nor should they; however, coaches should strive to develop a comprehensive understanding of where each team is functioning in relation to the indicators in the strategy implementation guide. Teams are more apt to be open to changes in practice when they know coaches have a deep understanding of their practice.

Providing Feedback

The journey to becoming a PLC involves cultural shifts. Richard DuFour and his colleagues (2016) call these shifts *reculturing*. Individual teams often begin their journey to becoming a PLC from different starting places. Teams that ignore the cultural shifts they need for a feedback-rich environment may struggle with the concepts of collaboration and continuous improvement. For some, collaboration around a common goal is a new experience. For others, the interdependence so crucial to a collaborative culture will mean learning or relearning new ways of working with others. Coaches can support teams in making these kinds of important shifts.

The kind of feedback that collaborative teams require will evolve over time. Thus, it is important that coaches be responsive to team members' developing expertise and needs. The feedback model that comes closest to supporting the differentiated needs of teams hangs on a continuum. Adapting from the work of Laura Lipton and Bruce Wellman (2001), we use the language of *consultant of task feedback, collaborator of conversational feedback*, and *coach of reflective feedback* to describe three ways or *stances* a coach might rely on as he or she interacts with teams implementing any of the practices of a PLC (C. Bryan, & B. Kaylor, personal communication, June 4, 2017).

In this model, coaches move the thinking and action of the team forward by operating within a continuum of different coaching stances. The simple diagram that follows (figure 4.1) illustrates three stances coaches can take when providing feedback to teams. In the diagram, the outlined figure symbolizes the coach; the shaded figures represent the team, with the larger of the figures designating who is responsible for leading the thinking and learning. Our belief is that feedback can and does occur in all three of these coaching stances.

Consultant
Task Feedback

Collaborator
Conversational Feedback

Coach
Reflective Feedback

Source: Adapted from Wellman & Lipton, 2001.

Figure 4.1: Feedback model for coaching teams.

We know that in every school there is a range of team effectiveness, and coaches need flexibility and versatility to shift among the stances of consultant, collaborator, and coach in order to promote learning and change.

With the right combination of feedback and coaching, teams are in good position to raise their performance and effectiveness to higher levels. Depending on the complexity of the new learning, it is not unusual for teams to move back and forth through various stages of learning as they implement new practices. Anticipating this possibility, coaches remain flexible, pay attention to various stances, and adjust the type of feedback they offer based on their observations, data, and team needs.

Consultant (Task) Feedback

In this role, the coach must wear the hat of the expert and operate in the role of consultant to help teams. The coach's feedback takes on a more directive tone as the coach may provide specific next steps teachers should take to improve the PLC process on their team. For example, a team might ask for feedback about how well it adheres to agreed-on norms. Some examples of norms teams might generate to help their meetings run efficiently and effectively include:

- Work from a set agenda.

- Create and use templates and protocols to organize meetings.

- Be present and engaged.

- Come prepared with appropriate products related to the outcome.

- Pose questions to seek understanding and challenge thinking.

- If a norm is broken, we will respond by _____.

In the role of consultant, the coach serves as a process observer, collects data throughout the meeting, and then shares his or her observations with the team. In the consultant role, the coach leads the team's thinking and learning by providing feedback in the form of objective data. He or she supports the team through modeling, providing exemplars, written or video resources, and even training when appropriate.

The following is an example of feedback a coach, with a consultant stance, might provide a team in a debrief session. This illustrates only part of the conversation, as it highlights the role of the coach, not team members.

"Thank you for letting me join your meeting today. I was excited to be part of your process. At today's collaborative team meeting, you wanted feedback about how posing questions enhanced your planning related to prioritizing the essential learning, specific skills, and conceptual understanding in your fractions unit. Would you like me to share my thinking? (Teachers agree.) Please remember that I'm here to provide you with feedback, based on my observations, that will strengthen your team. I'm not evaluating you, but instead I'm acting as a supporter.

"Let's get started. Over the course of the fifty-minute planning session, two probing questions were asked in a row about twenty minutes into the meeting. For example, one team member asked the probing question, 'Didn't this essential standard come up several times throughout the year last year? When does it have to be mastered?' This question prompted the group to pause and reflect. Another team member said, 'I hadn't considered that and the timeline. Maybe it is not a priority at this time.'

"Because of the probing question, you were able to reach consensus that you could wait to teach it later in the year. The remaining time was spent with each team member advocating for each of their ideas. At several points in the planning, team members were

not listening to each other and waiting to jump in with their own ideas; at that point, team members were not hearing each other.

"You need to strengthen your team's ability to listen to and pose questions to one another. By doing so, you will increase your team's effectiveness, but you've got to work on it. Consider assigning a process observer from your team who will provide data and feedback related to your goal."

Collaborator of Conversational Feedback

Other times, a coach rolls up his or her sleeves and works side-by-side in collaboration with a team of teachers. Using this same scenario of a team wanting feedback about how well it adheres to its norms, the team and coach, working together, choose one norm at the beginning of the meeting to focus on. At the conclusion of the meeting, the team self-assesses and sets a new goal. As a collaborator, the coach partners with the team to co-think, co-create, brainstorm, problem solve, or engage in inquiry thinking (conversational feedback). In conversations such as these, "Learners and their learning partners [coaches] collaboratively analyze data, generate learning from their analysis, and plan next actions" (Killion, 2015, p. 16). The following is an example of feedback a coach, with a collaborator stance, might provide a team after observing the team meeting. This illustrates only part of the conversation, as it highlights the role of the coach, not team members.

"Everyone, thanks for inviting me to join you today. I am impressed by your team's ability to reach consensus regarding your prioritized standards.

"As you asked, today I am collecting notes on the norm of posing questions. After spending time with you in your team meeting, I have observed that you have worked on posing questions. During today's planning session, there were more questions and more interaction among the team. In fact, I recorded nineteen questions during today's meeting. Asking questions to clarify and probe thinking shows you are working toward higher levels of implementation.

"I also noticed that the nineteen questions were not evenly attributed to team members. Instead, the total number of questions asked were: Julie—four, Robert—two , Tania—nine, and Keelan—four.

"How might you work to distribute time for asking questions more evenly among group members? What strategies do you use with students to ensure fairly equal participation? Would any of the strategies work for you? How will you monitor a plan to ensure a better balance of questions during your next planning meeting?

(The team begins to discuss and reaches consensus on their next steps.)

Coach of Reflective Feedback

A coach of reflective feedback provides teams with ongoing opportunities to make meaning of their practice. A coach should choose this role as often as possible; it is this stance that most deeply supports the team's development and thinking. A coach of reflective feedback poses questions that provoke reflection and deepen learning so he or she can mediate the team's thinking.

Continuing with the example of examining adherence to norms, a team might provide its own feedback through self-reflection with the support of a coach who provides the structure of time and thought-provoking questions. The following is an example of feedback a coach, in the stance of a coach of reflective feedback, might provide a team during a debriefing of their team meeting. This illustrates only part of the conversation, as it highlights the role of the coach, not team members.

> *"As you reflect on today's collaborative meeting, what did you notice in relation to your chosen norm, 'posing questions?" Did you notice any changes in group dynamics when members posed questions? If so, what did you notice? If not, what was a barrier? What are your next steps as a team?"*

Teams that become extremely successful often achieve high levels of effectiveness because they welcome feedback and have come to expect it as a part of the process of continuous improvement. As teams become more productive and proficient, they are better able to adapt to the complexities of the task at hand, operate with the maximum levels of efficiency and efficacy, and have structures in place that foster extraordinary levels of collaboration. They regularly take note of their progress and celebrate small wins. These teams naturally seek support from each other, coaches, administrators, and experts from outside the school or district.

All teams have room for improvement; the difference between them is that high-performing teams often already know they need to adjust and typically seek solutions on their own. They are the first to tell you they do not need the principal or coach telling them what to do, nor do they need a content or process expert to show them a better way. What these teams really need is someone who will listen, seek to understand the situation, and ask mediating questions. For teams at this level, the most effective coach is one who fosters self-reflection by the team before prioritizing and identifying next steps.

As observers of many collaborative teams working in PLCs, we stress the importance of making sure all individuals on a team understand that collecting data and providing feedback are a natural part of a cycle of continuous improvement.

"Feedback is not advice, praise or evaluation. Feedback is information about how we are doing in our efforts to reach a goal" (Wiggins, 2012, p. 10); feedback allows teams to make connections and adjust their practice.

Applying Feedback

Coaches also need to ensure that teams have time to make sense of the feedback and apply new learning to their work. It's not rare to hear a team of teachers exclaim, "We barely had the chance to talk about the feedback from last week!" Coaches should carefully consider the timing and amount of feedback they provide. A deliberate pause in the process is important, with no other suggestions, recommendations, or information given until teams agree on how they plan to respond to the feedback they've already received; otherwise, teams may feel bombarded with feedback. For feedback to be effective, the team must understand and accept it.

The best coaches diagnose where teams are in the process of developing into highly effective collaborative teams. Coaches then begin to differentiate their feedback based on which of the roles (stances) they think best reflects the team's current level of development.

Figure 4.2 (pages 77–78) provides sample team actions that can help coaches choose an appropriate feedback stance.

Data Stems

Data stems are universal and not specific to any feedback stance. A coach can use data stems as a natural way to bring objective data into the team coaching conversation. When coaches introduce data that are connected to the SIG, they provide a clear baseline of current practice.

Figure 4.2 shows sample data stems.

Feedback Stems

Choosing the best possible feedback stem depends on the feedback stance a coach chooses. Feedback stems are more directive (task level) in nature if the coach assumes a consultant stance, more suggestive if the coach operates from a collaborator stance, and more reflective when operating from a reflective stance. Use of feedback stems cultivates partnership while creating opportunity for rich dialogue between the coach and team as both parties deepen learning and push to reach consensus on next steps.

Figure 4.2 provides sample feedback stems.

	Team Actions	Data Stems	Feedback Stems	Next Steps
Consultant Task Feedback	• Is unaware of current practice and next steps • Is not receiving or attempting to apply new information and content • Is in the early stages of skill acquisition • Has a limited degree of proficiency • Is using practice that is unacceptable	• "Based on the observation data you collected . . ." • "From your time together, the team demonstrated . . ." • "During this collaborative planning, the group exhibited . . ." • "As we look at the SIG, here are the evident indicators . . ."	• "It is important that the team . . ." • "The team needs to . . ." • "In order to be effective, the team must . . ." • "As we think about implementation related to acceptable practice, the team should . . ." • "A next step for the team is . . ."	• Choose next practice from an indicator in the SIG and pathways tools that defines the team's prioritized next steps for improvement. • Show the next prioritized step or steps
Collaborator Conversational Feedback	• Is approaching acceptable practice • Is already operating at a level of acceptable practice and can benefit from suggestions to enhance effectiveness • Is honing new skills	• "As we look at the data, here are the evident indicators . . ." • "Throughout your team interaction, these elements from the SIG or data were visible . . ."	• "How are you ensuring . . .?" • "What would happen if . . .?" • "What could you anticipate if . . .?" • "What ways could you have . . .?" • "Might you consider . . .?" • "How might shifting _____ support the team to increase _____?"	
Coach Reflective Feedback	• Is calibrated and self-aware • Demonstrates highly effective practice • Looks to transfer practice to other content and work	• "During this collaborative team meeting, the highlighted areas represent the SIG indicators the team demonstrated . . ."	• "Based on _____, what are the team's thoughts moving forward?" • "How might the team apply this to other collaborative planning in _____? (content area) • "How is the team thinking about applying . . .?" • "What adjustments are you considering . . .?" • "What are you thinking about in relation to implementation?" • "What is your next step?"	

As a consultant, say:

- "During your team meetings, you remain off topic; to address this, the team should establish norms, keep them visible, and consistently refer to them throughout meetings to guide your efforts."

- "Your team consistently identifies the essential standards you expect students to master. However, you need to develop and administer common assessments so you can begin to compare which classroom teaching practices are more effective for your students."

- "As a team, you identified learning targets for past units. However, there is a discrepancy in expectations among team members. Moving forward, it is important that you agree on proficiency levels for the learning targets."

As a collaborator, say:

- "Your team has established norms and roles that you revisit and apply in every collaborative team meeting. How might developing collective commitments keep your team accountable and on track?"

- "As a team, you have identified essential standards for the last unit. Moving forward, how might establishing prerequisite skills benefit students so you can front-load them for success?"

- "As a team, you consistently create common formative assessments. How are you ensuring that you collaborate around common scoring?"

As a coach of reflective thinking, say:

- "As a team, you use protocols extensively to keep your conversations focused on students. What are your thoughts on how you will bring your new teammates on board next year with this practice?"

- "As a team, you have collaboratively identified the learning targets and proficiency levels for this unit. What are your thoughts on how you will vertically align them with other grade levels?"

- "As a team, how can you apply the successes you have had developing mathematics common formative assessments as you begin writing common formative assessments for reading?"

Figure 4.2: Ideas to deliver effective feedback to teams by coaching stance.

*Visit **go.SolutionTree.com/PLCbooks** for a free reproducible version of this figure.*

Next Steps

Coaches can help teams come to consensus and prioritize what they need to do next to continue improving. Naming a team's next step or steps using terminology from the SIG clarifies a focus area and commits coaches and teams to a single, unifying goal. This simple act of identifying next steps using common language from the SIG helps to lock in agreements, commitments, and timelines for both parties.

Figure 4.2 provides some ideas to help coaches shape their thinking when planning to deliver feedback to teams. Coaches can use the language of data stems, feedback stems, and next steps to frame specific feedback from each role of the feedback continuum. To support collaborative conversations, the stems anchor feedback in data to determine the next steps (the pathway) the team must take.

Some individuals and teams are uncomfortable receiving feedback; it can be an intimidating experience—even for veteran teachers. Individuals may personalize the feedback and become defensive. The best way to prevent this from happening is to ensure that coaches ground feedback in objective data. As coaches offer feedback, it is important that they connect the conversation to the team's SIG (see chapter 3, page 47) and the pathways—how teams will address each critical question of a PLC. (See chapter 5, page 85, for a thorough discussion of the pathways tool.) Feedback is the bridge that allows the coach to link clarity and support.

Connecting Feedback to the SIG

As teams progress to higher and higher levels of effectiveness, we have observed firsthand the power of providing teams with purposeful, ongoing feedback. Coaches create a powerful prescription for improving teaching and learning with frequent feedback, delivered at the right level and right time, that is clarified with data collected and correlated to a SIG that represents an agreed-on standard of best PLC practice. This is one of the fundamental components of coaching collaborative teams. Coaches amplify the impact of feedback on teaching and learning when feedback:

- **Fosters clarity and promotes collective action**—Effective feedback helps teams determine next steps and encourages the creation of action plans to improve learning.

- **Reduces variability between and among classrooms**—Teachers recognize that when they improve their PLC practices, teaching and learning improve as well.

- **Diminishes feelings of vulnerability**—The team, not individuals, receives feedback.

- **Allows teams to calibrate their practice**—Teams calibrate their understanding of a high-functioning, collaborative team.

If feedback relies on perception, without the use of objective data, teams may perceive the feedback as biased. We have found several strategies to support the gathering of data, but the best is to use a SIG. Experience shows us that if the SIG is the road map outlining where teams need to go, then feedback is the vehicle for moving teams forward. Teachers are more likely to respond favorably to feedback that is anchored in a set of agreed-on standards of best practice. Using a SIG to gather data about a team's level of PLC implementation promotes clarity and more effective collaboration. According to Kraft et al. (2017), "Building environments where providing and receiving constructive feedback is a regular part of teachers' professional work may be a key condition for the success of scale-up efforts [of coaching initiatives]" (p. 32). Teams maximize the benefits of feedback in a collaborative culture with continuous improvement, interdependence, and results. Collaborative cultures that value feedback are not random or accidental occurrences, and, in the end, the advantages of coaching teams far outweigh the disadvantages.

Learning From a Case Study on the Impact of Feedback

From 2010 through 2015 Jeffco Schools implemented a federal Teacher Incentive Fund (TIF) grant through the U.S. Department of Education in 20 of the 154 schools across the district (U.S. Department of Education, 2015). A major goal for the pilot was to improve student achievement through enhancing the quality of feedback individual teachers received.

As part of the grant, an independent research firm gathered data on student achievement and teacher effectiveness. The researchers completed annual program evaluations of the grant's activities and identified practices that required adjustment.

Based on the firm's findings, district leaders continuously fine-tuned the feedback process principals and coaches used to improve an individual teacher's classroom practice. The grant experience created a robust teacher-observation system that included feedback and support from instructional coaches. As a result, pilot schools in Jefferson County, those identified as high-implementing schools, saw improvement in student achievement (as measured on benchmark testing) and teacher effectiveness (as measured on district-evaluation rubrics), and over 80 percent of teachers reported that their instructional practices improved because of the feedback and coaching support they received (American Institutes for Research, 2016).

During the five years of the grant, district leaders, principals, and coaches noticed two trends in the data: student achievement improved in schools in which (1) principals and instructional coaches implemented an aligned system of clarity, feedback, and support and (2) collaborative teams focused on improving their PLC practices. After reviewing these data, district leaders decided to place a greater emphasis on implementing the PLC process and shifting some of their coaching support from individual teachers to collaborative teams.

The district drew on what it had learned about the importance of clarity, feedback, and support to individual teachers and applied those insights to collaborative teams within a PLC. Jeffco leaders began to explore the notion that while these data showed that feedback and support benefit individual teachers, applying a similar approach to collaborative teams working in PLCs might generate even better results.

The twenty pilot schools created a learning network and scheduled monthly meetings for ongoing professional development. The network offered an opportunity for celebration and problem solving while district administrators, building principals, and teacher leaders worked to apply what they had learned about coaching individual teachers to coaching collaborative teams. Just as they had discovered when working with individual teachers, leaders in Jeffco determined that for feedback to be effective, it needed to be an ongoing process, and they announced their intention to shift some of their coaching resources from individual teachers to collaborative teams.

Figure 4.3 (page 82) depicts the five-step process Jeffco schools used to gather observational data and deliver effective feedback to collaborative teams. The five steps proved to be essential to the success of team coaching in Jefferson County.

To ensure teams were clear about expectations, Jeffco principals and coaches developed a SIG (which they called a PLC Implementation Continuum) that served as the agreed-on standard across all twenty schools. Faculty and staff attended additional training to create a common understanding of the SIG contents and agreed on how coaches would use it as an improvement tool.

After designing the SIG, principals and coaches spent time honing their observation and data-collection skills. Professional development opportunities concentrated on how to collect neutral data anchored to various indicators on the SIG. Another round of training emphasized the importance of being nonjudgmental and using only neutral data when debriefing with collaborative teams.

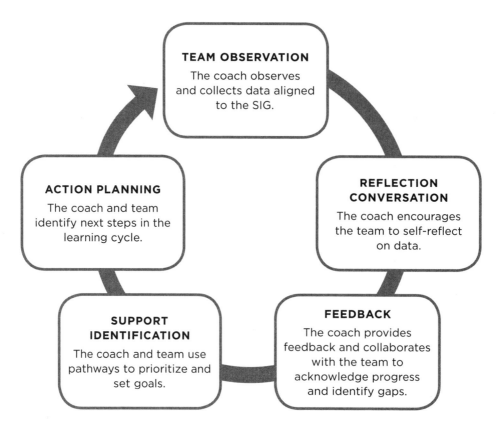

Figure 4.3: Five-step process for obtaining data and giving feedback.

After observing a collaborative team meeting in which administrators and coaches reviewed artifacts and collected data, teams scheduled an opportunity to talk and reflect on what team members observed. Teams found these conversations beneficial as they focused on observation data grounded in the SIG's anchor statements, indicators, and descriptors.

During these reflective conversations, administrators, coaches, and teams took time to celebrate progress in relation to the SIG, identify existing gaps, and explore opportunities for future team growth. Within months, district leaders noted that the opportunity for feedback led to greater ownership of the PLC process at the school sites.

Because of these opportunities for feedback, instructional coaches and collaborative teams moved deeper into the process and worked to focus on an action plan for the one area of the SIG that the team struggled with the most. The process of setting goals and prioritizing next steps allowed everyone to work toward common, defined outcomes. As teams identified gaps and set goals, they also identified potential ways coaches could support teams. The pathways tool (see chapter 5, page 85, for more information) helped the teams and coaches articulate the specific level and type of support they needed to improve.

Jefferson County's story of clarity, feedback, and support for teams continues. Since starting with the twenty pilot schools associated with the original grant, more than one hundred other schools from across the district have voluntarily joined the project. They are part of a cohort of schools that engage in professional learning and support to deepen their understanding of the PLC process. (Visit the Jeffco Schools website [goo.gl/a7dJmS] to learn more about the district's PLC journey.)

Conclusion

Feedback provides the bridge between clarity and support, and the act of delivering effective feedback is a critical component of coaching teams. Feedback is most effective when grounded in an agreed-on standard of best practice (the SIG) and differentiated based on the needs of teams (with the consultant, collaborator, or coach stance).

In chapter 5, we explore the third aspect of our coaching framework: support. Chapter 5 introduces the pathways tool and illustrates how coaches use it to support the work of collaborative teams within a PLC.

CHAPTER 5

Amplifying Your Impact
With Support

A positive school culture is a place where . . . educators create
policies and procedures and adopt practices that support
their belief in the ability of every student.

—ANTHONY MUHAMMAD

So far, we have discussed how to help collaborative teams create a SIG to clarify their vision, and we described why providing teams with feedback about their development is so important in helping them become more effective. Eaker and Dillard (2017) find that:

> Helping collaborative teams perform at a high level requires recognition of the fact that adults, like students, learn at different rates. . . . For leaders of PLCs, this means that some teams will require more, and different, additional time and support in order to continually improve the quality of their collaborative efforts. (p. 47)

This chapter focuses on the pathways for coaching collaborative teams in a PLC, which provide collaborative teams with differentiated support and increase their effectiveness in answering the four critical questions of a PLC (DuFour et al., 2016): (1) What do we want students to know and be able to do? (2) How will we know if they learned it? (3) What will we do if they didn't learn it? (4) What will we do for students who have already learned the material? In this chapter, we feature a pathways tool that focuses on each critical question.

Using Pathways for Coaching Collaborative Teams in a PLC

While the purpose of coaching collaborative teams is ultimately to increase student achievement, there are intermediary steps to achieving that goal that must take place. In order for a team to effectively increase achievement, team members must continually utilize their collaborative time to answer the four critical questions of a PLC. Many teams, however, do not use their collaborative time for that purpose. In *Team to Teach: A Facilitator's Guide to Professional Learning Teams*, Anne Jolly (2008) contends that team discussions often get off track or turn into *gripe sessions*, and that conversation guides are a necessary tool to keep teams moving forward. The National School Reform Faculty (Harmony Education Center, 2014) also recommends the use of protocols so that teams use collaborative time effectively. Collaborative teams in the East Detroit Public Schools needed support in using collaborative time effectively, so the district developed a conversation guide for collaborative teams. This guide has since been developed into the Pathways for Coaching Collaborative Teams in a PLC, which helps collaborative teams focus on matters of teacher reflection and student achievement. The tool is composed of matrices with a series of questions that focus on a different aspect of each of the four critical questions. By collaboratively discussing the answers to the four critical questions with a coach's guidance, teams receive the support they need to deepen their understanding of the PLC process and move forward in the instructional learning cycle.

Before East Detroit began utilizing the pathways tool, it had already laid much groundwork in its PLC transformation using a series of workshops designed around the text *Leverage* (2015). Grade-level teams used Larry Ainsworth's (2004) protocol for prioritizing standards and verified their decisions using the Surveys of Enacted Curriculum (SEC) documents for the Common Core State Standards (available on the CCSSO website [http://bit.ly/2wRzi5m]). (Visit **go.SolutionTree.com /PLCbooks** to access live links to the websites mentioned in this book.)

From there, teams unwrapped each priority standard to reveal specific learning targets. Some of the richest conversations came from creating a summary document that required teams to agree on a definition of proficiency, prerequisite skills, and common vocabulary for each priority standard. This activity gave teams the opportunity to create consistent expectations for members by creating a deep understanding of each priority standard and what it would look like when students had learned it.

Teams also had time over the summer, with the support of instructional coaches, to retool their reading units and create both summative and formative common assessments based on the priority standards. These assessments would become the lynchpin of each unit, assessing students' progress toward mastering the priority standards. Of most importance, however, was the way in which teachers analyzed the formative and summative assessment data so they would have specific information about each student's strengths and weaknesses as well as direction on what next steps to take to improve instruction.

With the groundwork firmly laid, teams met weekly to answer the four critical questions of a PLC using a pathways tool focused on each critical question. During each meeting, teams determined which path to follow based on their location in the instructional learning cycle and their students' needs. Coaches were instrumental in helping teams decide which path made the most sense for them at that point in time. Utilizing the pathways tool allowed coaches to differentiate their feedback based on each individual team's needs. Some teams started off needing directives from coaches, which were rooted in the pathways. Other teams, however, were further along in their thinking and needed coaches to work with them side by side. In cases such as these, coaches used the pathways tool as a guide for developing probing questions and initiating deeper conversations about the topics. See figure 5.1 (pages 88–89) for the original pathways tool (titled PLC Meeting Guidance) that was used in East Detroit.

This guide was originally created to provide general support and direction for collaborative teams (see figure 5.1, pages 88–89); however, we advocate creating much more specific pathways that delve into each critical question of a PLC. Figure 5.2 (page 90) breaks down each of the four critical questions of a PLC and identifies a revised pathways tool that helps address each one. The pathways flow down the chart from each critical question listed at the top. These thirteen actions (prioritizing standards, creating common formative assessments, analyzing strategies, planning enrichment activities, and so on) are based on the general steps needed to complete an instructional learning cycle in a PLC, and each has a corresponding pathway that coaches and teams use to move through the process. Again, schools and districts can adapt the pathways to more closely reflect the actions and language unique to their own school or district.

It is important to note that each team meeting should begin with a review of a SMART (strategic and specific, measurable, attainable, results oriented, and time bound; Conzemius & O'Neill, 2014) goal so that teams have a common understanding of what they are trying to achieve and will be able to recognize when they reach that goal. Coaches help teams identify which of the four questions they are working on at that point in the unit and guide teams through the pathways for that particular question. The level of support depends, of course, on the team and members' level of need. In the sections that follow, we examine the pathways for each critical question of a PLC. Please keep in mind that these are examples, and that schools and districts can benefit by collaboratively creating their own pathways specific to the language and practices in their own district.

PLC Meeting Guidance

Implement the following pathways after teams prioritize standards, identify learning targets, and determine proficiency definitions. Teams choose which path or paths to follow according to the pacing of instruction, student needs, and team next steps. Review SMART goals and answer the following questions.

Unit Planning	Identifying Strategies	Creating Common Formative Assessments (CFAs)	Analyzing Student Work	Analyzing Assessment Data
What targets will you be working on next?	What instructional strategies did you use for each target?	When will you administer your new CFA?	What student work samples did you bring to discuss as a team? What target or targets does this student work address?	What assessment data did you bring to discuss as a team?
Approximately how much time will you spend teaching each target? To what level of rigor (DOK)?	Which ones worked well? How do you know?	What targets will you address on this CFA? What targets from previous instruction do you need to reassess?	Find examples of student work you deem proficient. What makes it proficient? Do you all agree?	What are the proficiency rates of each target in individual classrooms? What are the overall team proficiency rates for each target you assessed?
What instructional strategies will best help students understand these targets? Which instructional strategies will you all agree to use between now and the next meeting?	Which ones didn't work well? How do you know?	What item types will best measure each target at the appropriate level of rigor? What mistakes do you expect students to make? How can you use those mistakes as distractors?	Look at the work of students who are not proficient. Are there common misconceptions or mistakes? How can you correct those misconceptions or mistakes?	What patterns or trends do you notice when looking at these data? What common misconceptions do you see?

What types of formative assessment will show whether students understand each target? Which formative assessments will you all agree to administer between now and the next meeting?	How can you alter these strategies to make them more successful?	What are the results of the assessment analysis your team conducted? What assessment alterations do you need to make?	Are there groups that outperformed others? Why? How can you transfer that success to other groups?	Are proficiency levels higher in some classes than others? Are there some successful strategies you can share with your colleagues?
What data, evidence, or student work should you all bring to the next meeting?	What other strategies should you try?	When will you analyze these CFA data as a team?	What should your next steps be as individual teachers and as a team?	How will your team address targets that need additional instruction? How will you address students who need intervention?

Concluding the meeting:

- What is the focus of your next meeting?

- What data, evidence, or student work will you all bring to the next team meeting?

Complete the meeting minutes and save them to the designated location.

Source: © 2017 Macomb Intermediate School District, Tesha Thomas. Reprinted with permission.

Figure 5.1: Pathways tool for coaching collaborative teams.

Visit go.SolutionTree.com/PLCbooks for a free reproducible version of this figure.

Critical Question One: What knowledge, skills, and dispositions should every student acquire as a result of this unit, this course, or this grade level?	Critical Question Two: How will we know when each student has acquired the essential knowledge and skills?	Critical Question Three: How will we respond when some students do not learn?	Critical Question Four: How will we extend the learning for students who are already proficient?
We're doing the following to answer this question:			
Prioritizing standards	Creating common formative assessments	Analyzing strategies (Teams will engage in similar practices at different stages of the instructional cycle, so there will be repeats.)	Planning enrichment activities
Identifying targets	Analyzing student work	Reviewing assessments	
Determining proficiency	Analyzing assessment data	Planning classroom interventions	
Planning units		Utilizing a system of support	
Analyzing strategies			

Figure 5.2: Revised pathways as they relate to the four critical questions of a PLC.

*Visit **go.SolutionTree.com/PLCbooks** for a free reproducible version of this figure.*

Pathways Tool for Critical Question One

Answering the first PLC question—What knowledge, skills, and dispositions should every student acquire as a result of this unit, this course, or this grade level?— lays the groundwork for all the others (DuFour et al., 2016). Teams must be clear about their goals for instruction in order for all teachers to deliver a guaranteed and viable curriculum. This can be an overwhelming task for teams new to the PLC process. There are a multitude of decisions that teams must make to adequately respond to this question. Coaches should support teams using the question one pathways (figure 5.3) as they navigate through very important conversations related to this question. The teams' responses to the pathways inquiries will help members determine the next steps they must take in the instructional learning cycle. The main actions for the first critical question include prioritizing standards, identifying targets, determining proficiency, planning units, and analyzing strategies.

Prioritizing Standards	Identifying Targets	Determining Proficiency	Planning Units	Analyzing Strategies
Which standards provide endurance?	What targets did the unwrapping process reveal?	How would you rewrite this target in student-friendly terms?	What targets will you be instructing on next?	What instructional strategies will you use?
Which standards provide readiness for the next level of learning?	Where does the current curriculum address these targets?	What are the prerequisite skills and vocabulary necessary to master this target?	What instructional strategies will you all agree to use during this unit?	Which strategies worked well when this unit was taught in the past? How do you know?
Which standards provide leverage?	Which targets are not adequately addressed in your current curriculum?	To what DOK level should students show mastery?	Approximately how much time will you spend teaching each target?	Which strategies did not work well last time this unit was taught? Why did they not work?
Which standards are most often assessed by standardized tests?	To what DOK level will you teach each target?	What will students create, produce, or be able to do when they master this target?	To what DOK level will you teach each target?	How can you alter these strategies to make them more successful?
If you could only teach ten standards in this course, which would they be? Why?	How will you pace your course curriculum to include these targets?	How will you grade or score this target?	What data, evidence, or student work should your team bring to the next meeting?	What strategies should you delete from this unit?
		What models of proficiency do you have or can you create?		What additional best-practice strategies should you try?

Figure 5.3: Pathways tool for critical question one.

*Visit **go.SolutionTree.com/PLCbooks** for a free reproducible version of this figure.*

Prioritizing Standards

In order for teams to respond to the first critical question of a PLC, teams must arrive at consensus when finalizing their list of high-priority standards. The tool for prioritizing standards follows a protocol Ainsworth (2003) references wherein teams methodically review each content standard one by one to determine if it:

- Provides students with endurance in the subject area over the long run
- Prepares students for the next grade level
- Offers students leverage in multiple subject areas
- Is likely a topic for assessment on standardized tests

Teams work together to agree on the standards that best meet these criteria and come to consensus on a list of priority standards. Sometimes this process can lead to disagreement among team members, but respectful disagreement can lead to new understanding and even strengthen the team's relationships if a coach mediates the disagreement skillfully. Arriving at consensus, where the will of the group is known (not necessarily a unanimous decision), is crucial in order for teams to take owner-ship of the prioritized standards. Coaches can assist by upholding team norms and using protocols for consensus building, such as the fist-to-five strategy (DuFour et al., 2016) where team members hold up their fingers (1–5) or a fist to indicate their level of agreement.

Identifying Targets

Once the team reaches consensus on the highest-priority standards, members must unwrap these standards to identify the specific learning targets within them. Most content-area standards contain multiple skills that teachers cannot teach simultane-ously. By breaking down the standard into discrete skills, teachers find the standards much more manageable, which allows them to focus their teaching on specific tar-gets rather than on trying to tackle the entire standard all at once. The pathway for identifying targets begins with an unwrapping process from Kim Bailey and Chris Jakicic (2012). This process asks teachers to identify the parts of speech within the standard to break it down into its most discrete skills. The following example (figure 5.4) shows how a team might use Bailey and Jakicic's (2012) method to unwrap the grade 6 Common Core Reading standard "Determine a theme or central idea of a text and how it is conveyed through particular details; provide a summary of the text distinct from personal opinions or judgments" (RL.6.2; National Governors Association Center for Best Practices [NGA] & Council of Chief State School Officers [CCSSO], 2010b).

Unwrapping Template

Focus on key words.

1. Circle all verbs (skills we expect students to be able to do).
2. Underline nouns (concepts students need to know).
3. Double underline any context clues (prepositional phrases).
4. Add any implied learning targets.

Standard: RL.6.2—Determine a theme or central idea of a text and how it is conveyed through particular details; provide a summary of the text distinct from personal opinions or judgments.

What Is the Target? (Name or Number)	What Will Students Do? (Skills or Verbs)	With What Knowledge or Concept? (Nouns or Direct Instruction)	In What Context?	What Level of Thinking Does It Involve?
Learning Target 1	Determine	a theme of a text	through particular details	DOK 2
Learning Target 2	Determine	the central idea of a text	through particular details	DOK 2
Learning Target 3	Determine	how a theme or central idea is conveyed	through particular details	DOK 2
Learning Target 4	Provide	a summary of the text	distinct from personal opinions or judgments	DOK 2
Foundational knowledge and concepts	Summarization vs. retelling; definitions of: theme, central idea, opinions, judgments, and facts.			
Foundational skills or processes	Summarizing; identifying theme or central idea; identifying key ideas, and details.			

Source for standard: NGA & CCSSO, 2010b.
Source: Adapted from Bailey & Jakicic, 2012.

Figure 5.4: Completed unwrapping template example.

Visit go.SolutionTree.com/PLCbooks for a free reproducible version of this figure.

Unwrapping standards can be a tricky process that requires interpretation and an understanding of the intent behind the standards. Not only can coaches help teams navigate through this process by walking them through the steps, but coaches with content knowledge can facilitate further discussion about dividing the standards based on the authors' intent, where the standards appear in the curriculum, and the best instructional strategies for delivering the material.

Once they identify the priority standard learning targets, teacher teams can focus on those specific targets to more easily plan their instructional units and daily lessons. Common formative and summative assessments are also easier to plan when they focus on specific learning targets. Furthermore, teams can turn targets into student-friendly *I can* statements or objectives so that students can take ownership over their own learning. When students understand the goal of the teacher's instruction, they are far more likely to achieve it.

Determining Proficiency

When teams come to consensus on a proficiency definition for each target and priority standard, grade-level and departmental collaboration becomes much more focused. It is impossible to determine if students reach mastery if teams do not clearly define mastery. Arriving at consensus for proficiency definitions, however, can be difficult to accomplish. Coaches can use the tool to guide teams through differing opinions and productive discourse about where students should be and at what mastery level they require. Conversations about prerequisite skills and vocabulary help solidify vertical alignment in the curriculum, while discussions on DOK (depth of knowledge) and cognitive rigor help teammates define their beliefs about levels of expectation. Identifying the end product students will complete to demonstrate mastery of the target and how teachers will assess it provide both teachers and students with a clear path toward reaching that target. It also provides a school with the foundation for a curriculum that is guaranteed and viable for all students, no matter to which teacher the school assigns them. These are powerful activities with far-reaching implications, and teams need support from coaches to ensure that all voices are heard and the team makes sound decisions.

Planning Units

We must be clear that unit planning in a PLC is different than a typical common planning period. Unit planning is not about identifying student activities or deciding on which day classes will read which book. It is about collaborative inquiry into which research-based strategies work best for which learning targets. It is about common pacing so that teachers deliver formative assessments at about the same time and then review comparative data as a team. It includes discussion about cognitive rigor and DOK levels for specific targets and the best ways to help students reach them.

Teams can benefit from coaches who question the effectiveness of instructional strategies, inquire into the timing of assessments, and nudge teachers to increase cognitive rigor levels in their activities. Some teams may never get to this level of discourse without the guidance of a coach.

However, teams and coaches must fully understand the goal is not identical daily lesson plans for all teachers on the team. Rather, it is about collectively using the best knowledge and experience of each individual team member to benefit all students in every class. Teachers should capitalize on their individual teaching style and learn what works best for their students—which won't be the same for every class. However, good teaching is good teaching. When we find strategies that are effective, we should be using them with all students. This is the hallmark of a true collaborative culture. While teachers are busy instructing in their own classrooms, coaches are often able to observe multiple classes teaching the same topics. This can lead to the identification of successful strategies and activities that might not otherwise be recognized or shared. Effective coaches identify the strengths of each team member and find ways to use them for the good of the group.

Analyzing Strategies

Once a team plans a unit and teachers begin instruction, it is important that the team reflects on the strategies it used in its lessons, whether or not these strategies were successful in helping students master the targets. This deep reflection can only happen when team members trust one another enough to make themselves vulnerable. Admitting that a strategy did not work can be a humbling experience for some teachers, and coaches must be aware of the feelings involved in admitting that things did not go as planned. A team will not be successful in this endeavor if members feel that their colleagues (or coach) are judging them. It is best to begin these conversations with a discussion about strategies that all teachers agreed to use within the unit.

By asking teachers to share their stories about how they implement a specific strategy and the impact on student learning, coaches can draw team members closer to each other through common experiences. On the other hand, it is crucial to capitalize on the *outliers*—teachers who have great success with a strategy when others do not. By identifying the differences in the ways such a teacher implements the strategy, the team can experiment and try again rather than simply discarding the strategy as unsuccessful. Team members may also discover through conversations with their teammates that a member uses a strategy that the others do not and ends up with more positive results. The rest of the team can then adopt the new strategy in lesson plans for future units.

It is important, though, that strategy analysis not stop at anecdotal experiences. It is no longer about whether students enjoy the activity; teachers must use hard data to prove that the strategies work. Yet data in the form of proficiency percentages need not be the only data teams use. Reviewing student work and identifying common areas of strength and weakness provides teams with extensive information on which strategies are most successful and which ones are not. Coaches can be an invaluable resource for teams analyzing student work, drawing attention to specific aspects that might otherwise be overlooked, and asking questions that force teams to dissect what students are and are not learning. (See the section Pathways Tool for Critical Question Two on page 97 of this chapter for a pathway on analyzing student work.)

Putting It All Together

Once the teams in East Detroit worked their way through the first question of a PLC—What do we want our students to know and be able to do?—as coaches, we felt it was important for teams to record their thinking for future reference. It was vital that any new teachers be able to quickly and easily locate and implement what colleagues had learned about their guaranteed and viable curriculum. Therefore, we created a summary document for each priority standard to communicate the basic ideas of the priority standard, including the unwrapped targets; student-friendly objectives; a description of proficiency; prerequisite skills and vocabulary; and planning information such as when teachers would address the standard throughout the year, how they would assess it, and ways to provide enrichment for students who already mastered the standard. It is important to note that there is no place in this document asking teams to identify strategies for intervention. This question is left out intentionally because East Detroit coaches feel teams should diagnose and treat individual students' specific needs when they are answering critical question three within the instructional learning cycle. However, other districts have revised this document to include the question, What will we do for students who have mastered the standard?

At East Detroit, all teachers receive hard copies of these documents for easy reference when planning lessons. Electronic copies appear with the district's curriculum units in an electronic warehouse. Of course, the summary document is not a final document; it's a constantly evolving tool teams review at the end of each unit and revise according to student needs. Figure 5.5 shows an example of a priority standard summary document.

Grade: __4__	Subject area: __Reading__
Priority standard: R.4.1: Refer to details and example in a text when explaining what the text says explicitly and when drawing inferences from the text.	**Planning** When will you teach this standard? • Unit 2 novel unit • Unit 3 informational text unit • Unit 5 research
Unwrapped targets: • Refer to details in a text when explaining what the text says explicitly. • Refer to examples in a text when explaining what the text says explicitly. • Refer to details in a text when drawing inferences. • Refer to examples in a text when drawing inferences.	What assessment or assessments will you use to measure student mastery? • Summary writing • Close and critical reading assignment • Details and examples to support topic sentence or thesis in literary analysis
Standard description (in student-friendly words): • I can identify details in a text when describing the plot of a story. • I can give examples of events in a text when describing the plot of a story. • I can identify the details of a text that help me make inferences. • I can give examples of events in a text that help me make inferences.	What will we do for students who have already mastered the essential standard? Work with these students to increase the DOK level of the assignment to a DOK 3. Examples: • Compare the inferred theme of two different stories.
Level of rigor or proficiency example: The student can write a summary of the story using specific details and examples to depict the main ideas, sequence of events, and inferred theme. (DOK 2)	• Write the summary from a character's point of view.
Prerequisite skills and vocabulary: • Details • Examples • Inferences • Plot • Main idea • Theme • Summary	

Source for standard: NGA & CCSSO, 2010a.

Figure 5.5: Sample priority standard summary document.

*Visit **go.SolutionTree.com/PLCbooks** for a free reproducible version of this figure.*

Pathways Tool for Critical Question Two

Schools and districts that adopt the PLC process transform their culture from a focus on teaching to a focus on learning. The focus of teacher teams should always be on which concepts students have learned. Once teachers know where their students stand in mastering the priority standards, they can collaboratively plan their next instructional moves. The best way to measure where students are in their mastery is to utilize regularly scheduled, short cycle, common formative assessments. Paul Black and Dylan Wiliam (1998) updated reviews of research by Gary Natriello (1987) and Terence J. Crooks (1988) to conclude that "regular use of classroom formative assessment would raise student achievement by 0.4 to 0.7 standard deviations—enough to raise the United States to the top five in international rankings" (as cited in Wiliam, 2007, p. 189). However, we can only achieve those results if we use formative assessment results to plan interventions that address specific student needs.

Accurately answering the second critical question—How do we know if our students have learned it?—depends on the team's ability to create assessments that measure specific targets of instruction at the DOK levels specified for proficiency. These assessments must provide teams with information that pinpoints exactly where student learning breaks down, so teams must design them with great forethought. While not all team members have adequate training in designing effective assessments, coaches can use the tool to assist teams in ensuring that common formative assessments diagnose specific student misconceptions. The collaborative development of these assessments will deepen teachers' knowledge of the standards and targets as well as the expected proficiency levels. As coaches guide teachers to predict student mistakes before instruction begins, teams proactively plan specific instructional strategies and identify interventions ahead of time. Once the assessments are delivered, coaches walk teams through analyzing student work and assessment data to identify misconceptions and make plans for next instructional steps. Please note that these two pathways purposely contain some of the same questions that are designed to encourage teams to reflect on their own instructional practices. The pathways that help teams answer critical question two (figure 5.6) covers creating common formative assessments, analyzing student work, and analyzing assessment data.

Creating Common Formative Assessments	Analyzing Student Work	Analyzing Assessment Data
When will you deliver your next CFA?	What student work samples did you bring to discuss as a team?	What assessment data did you bring to discuss as a team?
What targets will you address in this CFA?	Find examples of student work you deem proficient. What makes them proficient? Do you all agree?	What are the proficiency rates of each target in individual classrooms?

What targets from previous instruction do you need to reassess?	Look at papers of students who are not proficient. Are there common misconceptions or mistakes? How can you correct those misconceptions or mistakes?	What are the overall team proficiency rates for each target you assessed?
At what DOK levels do you expect students to master the target? Do the CFA questions match this expected level of DOK?	Look at the questions most students got wrong. What are the patterns among the wrong answers? How can you correct the misconceptions or mistakes?	Are proficiency levels higher in some classes than in others? Why? How can you transfer that success to other classes?
What question types will best measure the students' mastery at the required DOK level? Are these included in your assessment?	Did some groups outperform others? Why? How can you transfer that success to other groups?	Which questions did the students most often get wrong? Why? What are the patterns among the wrong answers? How can your team correct the misconceptions or mistakes?
Are there enough items per target to accurately measure the student's level of mastery?	What connections can you make between student performance and instructional strategies?	What connections can you make between student performance and instructional strategies?
Do your multiple-choice items include distractors that will help you identify specific misconceptions?	How will your team address targets that need additional whole-class instruction?	How will your team address targets that need additional whole-class instruction?
When will you analyze the CFA data as a team?	Which students need interventions on which targets? What is your plan for providing those students with additional instruction?	Which students need interventions on which targets? What is your plan for providing those students with additional instruction?
	What should your next steps be as a classroom teacher? As a team?	What adjustments do you need to make to the assessment?

Figure 5.6: Pathways for critical question two.

*Visit **go.SolutionTree.com/PLCbooks** for a free reproducible version of this figure.*

Creating Common Formative Assessments

Formative assessment is one of the most powerful strategies a teacher can use—if he or she acts on the data from the assessment (Fullan, 2005). To truly get the most out of formative assessments, the teacher must also share results with his or her students. According to superintendent and author Eric Twadell (2015) students need to ask themselves three questions every day: "What am I supposed to be learning? Where am I in my learning? What do I need to do to close the gap?" (p. 6). Formative assessment feedback provides both students and their teachers with knowledge of where students are in their learning so that they can make plans to close the gap.

In order for formative assessments to provide specific information on where the student is in his or her learning, teams must design the assessments for that purpose. Teams must be strategic about which targets they are assessing and when. The tool for developing common formative assessments guides teams through questions that will lead them toward the creation of assessments that are both valid and reliable, as well as specific enough to diagnose student needs.

To ensure validity, teams must test the specific targets on which they instruct students. Not all targets are created equally, so teams must return to their prioritized standards and summative assessment to determine which targets merit formative assessment. Of course, teams should decide on this before instruction takes place. Validity not only requires that teams assess the priority targets they teaches, but teams must assess those targets at the cognitive rigor or DOK level that the team determines is necessary for proficiency. To help in this, the questions in the pathways tool ask teams to consider the types of assessment items they are using and whether they best measure the required cognitive rigor or DOK level. Coaches can help teams create items that assess the same target in multiple ways. In so doing, teachers can experience firsthand the ways in which different item types can adjust cognitive rigor levels.

In addition, all assessments must be reliable in order for teachers to be confident in the results. The tool asks teams to consider the number of questions teachers include for each target. Typically, three to five selected-response items will adequately measure whether a student masters a particular target. Teams must also consider the number of points they assign to each item and each target in order to ensure a fair balance for grading purposes. Teams can discuss the amount of time spent on the target, the amount of emphasis on that target, and the target's level of importance to determine the number of points for each object. No matter the decision, it is imperative that the collaborative team reach consensus so there is consistency in grading. Coaches are extremely helpful in guiding teams through this discussion, which can be difficult. While the topic of grading can be a source of disagreement, healthy disagreement can strengthen teams and provide opportunities for teachers to stretch their thinking.

The final question in this pathway relates to an assessment item's wrong answers—otherwise known as *distractors*. When written carefully, the distractors students choose as answers can tell teachers a great deal about where students are in their learning. To make assessment items effective, teachers must predict student misconceptions and the mistakes those misconceptions cause. By including those mistakes as distractors on the assessment, teams can analyze data to determine which students possess specific misconceptions. Teams and their coaches can then work together to plan and deliver interventions for specific students that address specific misconceptions.

Analyzing Student Work

Another method of responding to the second critical question of a PLC is through collaborative analysis of student work. Collaboratively reviewing student answers can help teams solidify the meaning of proficiency and lead to discussions on strategies for helping students reach it. Identifying patterns among student answers can reveal the specific point where student thinking breaks down, leading to wrong answers. This is the goal of common formative assessment. When teachers can identify the exact point at which student thinking breaks down, they can provide students with the specific interventions to get them headed along the right path once again. It is important that teams do not stop at simply identifying patterns among student answers. Like the pathway for analyzing student work, this pathway intentionally poses questions that require teams to think about the connections between their students' answers and the instructional strategies they use in the classroom. The goal is for teachers to reflect on their instruction and decide whether the levels of student learning deem those practices as successful. The additional support and probing from coaches can only serve to deepen teacher reflection.

Finally, like the previous pathway, teams and coaches must work together to create a specific plan to meet student weaknesses once analysis of student work has diagnosed these needs. We cannot overstate these plans' importance, which we discuss further in the section on critical question three. (See Pathways Tool for Critical Question Three on page 102.)

Analyzing Assessment Data

The pathway for analysis of assessment data is similar to the pathway for analyzing student work; the goal of both is to identify student misconceptions so teams can intervene as quickly as possible. Teams must disaggregate data to the student level so that teachers can make individual diagnoses with specific plans for intervention. It is also important that coaches work with teams to compare data between classes to identify any strategies that are especially successful and make plans to replicate them in other classes. While comparing results can be uncomfortable in a team setting, it is important that teachers discuss varying results to identify effective practices. Coaches can help encourage collaborative inquiry and build trusting relationships among team members to ease this discomfort.

Finally, coaches assisting teams with this pathway should guide teachers through a critical examination of the assessment itself. When teams look at the items that most students got wrong, they often find problems with the way in which they ask a question, the vocabulary they use, or even distractors that students could consider correct answers. This provides teams with an opportunity to improve the assessment for the following school year and should serve as a warning that the same errors could exist in other team-developed assessments that have not been delivered yet. Hopefully, coaches and teams use this information to review future assessments and correct errors. One warning regarding this component of the pathway: focusing on assessment items is safer for teachers than reflecting on their own instructional practices. While analyzing the assessment is a necessary activity, it is crucial that teams not get stuck there. Coaches are instrumental in moving teams through this portion of the pathways tool while maintaining an emphasis on student learning and a reflection on teacher practices.

Pathways Tool for Critical Question Three

While critical question two asks teams to analyze common assessment results, the power of that analysis comes through the ways in which teams respond to those results. Unfortunately, it is easy for teams to get mired in these data. After all, discussing numbers is far less threatening than reflecting on one's own practices.

Teams in East Detroit have committed to reviewing their individual classroom data before each team meeting so they can spend team time discussing collective results and planning interventions. In fact, East Detroit leaders have set goals for teams to spend 25 percent of their meeting time discussing numbers and 75 percent making plans for intervention. Coaches utilizing the pathways can keep teams focused on instruction and intervention rather than spending too much time "admiring" the data.

Deciding on strategies to intervene with students who did not master the priority standards or targets can be difficult. Most teachers gave it their "best shot" the first time around, so they often struggle to find new ways of reteaching the same content. This is what makes a collaborative culture so impactful. Collaborative team members can do far more together than they ever could alone. As assessment expert Thomas Guskey (2009) states:

The best ideas for effective corrective activities—interventions—generally come from fellow teachers. Teaching colleagues often can offer new ways of presenting concepts, different examples, and alternative materials. Professional opportunities that provide teachers with time for such sharing reduce the workload of individual teachers and typically yield higher quality activities. (p. 29)

Coaches can use the pathways tool to lead teams to collaboratively plan intervention strategies not only for individual classrooms, but for entire grade levels of students. For example, at Bellview Elementary in East Detroit, the fourth-grade team implemented *Intervention Fridays*. The team utilizes common formative assessment results to intentionally group all students in the grade level according to deficit areas. Using the pathways as a guide, the team then creates an intervention plan for each deficit area, and each teacher works with a group of students to implement the planned interventions.

The pathways tool for responding to critical question three (figure 5.7, page 104) includes pathways for analyzing strategies, reviewing assessments, planning classroom interventions, and utilizing a system of supports. These might include a multitiered system of supports (MTSS), response to intervention (RTI), or a pyramid of interventions. Although these terms are not interchangeable, they all include the common purpose of identifying struggling students early on and providing them with systemic interventions.

RTI's underlying premise is that schools should not wait until students fall far enough behind to qualify for special education to provide them with the help they need. Instead, schools should provide targeted and systematic interventions to all students as soon as they demonstrate the need (Buffum, Mattos, & Weber, 2010).

These support systems typically consist of three tiers:

- Tier 1 instruction that all students receive
- Tier 2 instruction for students who have difficulty mastering essential material; instruction targeted toward specific student needs or weaknesses (in addition to Tier 1 instruction)
- Tier 3 intervention for students who require a more intensive level of instruction to master the essential material; delivered with increased intensity, duration, and frequency (in addition to Tier 1)

Analyzing Strategies	Reviewing Assessments	Planning Classroom Interventions	Utilizing a System of Supports
What instructional strategies did you use?	Which questions do students most commonly answer wrong?	What DOK level constitutes proficiency? At what DOK level did students perform?	Has this student been identified to receive Tier 2 or Tier 3 support?
Which ones work well? How do you know?	What standards and targets do those questions assess?	What pieces of the content are students missing (specific targets)?	What type of support is this student already receiving within the classroom?
Which ones didn't work well? How do you know?	What vocabulary in the question and answers could trip up your students?	How can you divide students into groups based on need?	What type of support is this student receiving outside the classroom?
How can you make these strategies more successful?	What patterns do you see in the distractors students chose? What common misconceptions can you identify?	How can you provide students with adjustments in the content you provide (lower Lexile materials, pictorial explanations, and so on)?	Does the student need additional Tier 2 or Tier 3 support?
What other strategies should you try?	Which targets need further small-group or whole-class instruction?	How can you provide students with a different process for understanding the material (for example, peer tutoring, cooperative learning, alternate readings, online activities, and so on)?	What next steps must you take to ensure this student is receiving all the support he or she needs?
	How can the classroom intervention pathway assist your team in making intervention plans?	Can students create a different kind of product to demonstrate their proficiency on this target?	
		How can you break down the material so students can experience success with the target?	

Figure 5.7: Pathways for critical question three.

*Visit **go.SolutionTree.com/PLCbooks** for a free reproducible version of this figure.*

Analyzing Strategies

The strategies analysis pathway asks teams to reflect on the specific strategies teachers use to teach each target and determine whether or not those strategies were successful. It is our hope that this pathway will result in team members sharing stories about the strategies they employ, using evidence to prove the strategy's success. However, it is also important for teams to identify the strategies that are unsuccessful and to figure out exactly why they don't work. Through these discussions, coaches can help teachers determine if the strategy is unsuccessful because teachers did not implement it with fidelity or whether it simply is not the appropriate strategy to teach the particular target. If the students do not learn the material because of a poor instructional choice, teachers need to not only provide an intervention but also ensure that they make a different choice in the future. It is crucial that coaches and team members build a level of trust so that honest reflection can take place, and mistakes can be seen as tools for learning.

Reviewing Assessments

As with the analyzing assessments pathway for critical question two, the goal of the reviewing assessments pathway is to determine if there are issues with the assessment that could negatively impact student performance. For example, if the test item includes vocabulary that may have confused students, teachers have two responsibilities: (1) intervene by teaching the vocabulary to the current group of students, and (2) preteach the vocabulary the following year or semester.

Identifying patterns among students' wrong answers can help teams determine if they have worded the questions in a confusing way, ineffectively taught a concept, or if students just need additional instruction and practice. If teams intentionally create the assessment to include distractors that would reveal specific student misconceptions, they can easily group students according to skill-deficit areas and provide them with the intervention they need. If teams do not intentionally include distractors to help identify where student thinking broke down, coaches can lead teams through the test review pathway to help them adjust the test accordingly.

Planning Classroom Interventions

The planning classroom interventions pathway is where teams identify exactly which targets students are missing and make a specific plan to intervene. However, simply reviewing the percentage correct on the assessment is not enough. Teams must also analyze students' levels of understanding to determine if they meet proficiency. While a student may meet the target at the memorization level (DOK 1), if the team determines proficiency is at application (DOK 3 or 4), additional instruction, practice, or intervention may be necessary.

When making a plan for student interventions, it is important for teachers to consider the ways in which they deliver the content, the process for delivering it, and the end product students use to demonstrate mastery (Tomlinson, 2001). For example, a student who reads far below grade level may score poorly on an assessment not because he or she doesn't understand the target but because the reading level of the assessment got in the way. To intervene in this case, a teacher could provide an alternate version of the assessment at a lower reading level or have the test read to the student. Providing these alternative content formats will help teachers obtain a more accurate read of the students' ability levels regarding the actual target. Coaches can be instrumental in helping teachers plan for differentiation, which is an instructional strategy that many teachers struggle to implement.

The area of intervention that teams most often address is the delivery process. Teams using the classroom intervention pathway should collaboratively consider the strategies they already use and identify new ways of delivering that content during intervention. Guskey (2009) states that in an effective intervention, the strategy must be different and engage students differently than the original delivery method, and it must provide students with opportunities for success. For example, if during initial instruction the teacher uses a whole-group learning activity and students do not master the target, the team can consider peer tutoring as an intervention strategy. The classroom interventions pathway provides teams with a list of possible delivery methods to consider when making intervention plans, although the list is certainly not exhaustive. Coaches and teams should regularly engage in collaborative inquiry to research and identify additional instructional strategies that will help deliver difficult material in new and different ways.

Finally, it is possible that students master the material but are not able to show it using the method of assessment teachers employed. Utilizing alternative methods of assessment allows students to showcase mastery levels that teachers might not have seen otherwise. Capitalizing on students' learning styles and modalities can provide teachers with a much more accurate assessment of student learning than a typical multiple choice, essay, or short-answer assessment. While most teachers are not extensively trained in assessment writing, coaches can guide teams through the creation of alternative assessments that not only provide a more accurate picture of students' learning but are often more rigorous and more engaging to students.

Utilizing a System of Supports

The final pathway for critical question three asks teams to consider the kinds of supports students are receiving in addition to classroom instruction. MTSS and RTI are schoolwide systems that educators implement at the building level. The system begins with a universal screening assessment for all students, with the goal of identifying any students who fall far below grade level in specific content areas. Struggling students then receive additional, systematic instruction with increased intensity to address *specific weaknesses.* As previously mentioned, this additional, systematic instruction (Tiers 2 and 3) is in addition to core (Tier 1) classroom instruction, and formal progress monitoring is conducted regularly to ensure students are receiving the support they need.

The pyramid of interventions introduced in *Whatever It Takes: How Professional Learning Communities Respond When Kids Don't Learn* (DuFour, DuFour, Eaker & Karhanek, 2004) is also designed to systematically provide struggling students with support, moving from least intensive to most intensive interventions as needed. Students in need of the services within the pyramid are often identified through the collaborative team's analysis of common formative and summative data. Coaches can be instrumental in helping teachers initiate this process and continuously monitor students' growth.

Teachers need to be acutely aware of the extra assistance their students are receiving and how it coincides with the instruction taking place within the classroom. It is vital, however, that all teachers understand that the first line of defense is always the classroom teacher. Tiers 2 and 3 interventions can never replace the core instruction and intervention that happens in the classroom on a daily basis. In the East Detroit schools, supplemental teachers who deliver interventions meet monthly with grade-level content-area teachers and coaches to share information about their students' progress. This provides both teachers with valuable information on the students' learning and allows them to collaboratively plan their next steps in moving the student forward.

Pathways Tool for Critical Question Four

The final critical question of a PLC asks teams to consider which students have already mastered the essential standards: How will we extend the learning for students who are already proficient? When large numbers of students need additional instruction, educators cannot hold back those students who have already mastered the material. Teachers must examine students' levels of mastery and provide opportunities for them to stretch their current thinking. They should consider the content, process, and products they are using to enrich student learning. Coaches can be helpful guiding teams as they collaboratively identify complex texts that will support the content and challenge students. A coach's guidance is also key as teams develop activities at higher-cognitive-rigor levels that allow students to dig deeper into the material. This can include asking students to apply their learning by teaching it to someone else, solving real-world problems, explaining the material from a different perspective, creating a model, or drawing conclusions and justifying those conclusions with evidence. See Karin Hess's (n.d.) webpage "Cognitive Rigor and Depth of Knowledge" (http://bit.ly/2u2QvHz) for matrices that cover multiple content areas. Coaches used these documents to assist East Detroit teachers as they planned for student enrichment activities. (Visit **go.SolutionTree.com/PLCbooks** to access live links to the websites mentioned in this book.)

See figure 5.8 for the pathways tool for helping teams answer the fourth critical question of a PLC.

Planning Enrichment Activities
What DOK level constitutes proficiency?   At what DOK level did your students perform?
What components of the content do your students understand the best (specific targets)?
What pieces of the content could you help your students stretch even further?
Are there students who need adjustments in the content you have provided (for example, higher-Lexile-level materials, and so on)?
How can you provide students with a different process for understanding the material at a deeper level (writing to learn, advance organizers, and so on)?
What different kinds of products (with a higher DOK) can students create to demonstrate their proficiency on this target?

Figure 5.8: Pathway for critical question four.

*Visit **go.SolutionTree.com/PLCbooks** for a free reproducible version of this figure.*

Conclusion

Employing the pathways for coaching collaborative teams in a PLC provides both coaches and teams with the sequential direction and structure they need to keep teams on track during collaborative meeting time and offers a common language for all school staff. The variety of pathways encourages coaches to differentiate the support they provide for each team according to its location in the instructional learning cycle. Finally, because the pathways are rooted in the four critical questions of a PLC, teams that work their way through these questions are far more likely to maintain their focus on the true work of PLCs.

Although teams without a coach could effectively use the pathways, engaging a coach in the process greatly enhances the positive effects of the tool. A coach helps teams see the bigger picture of PLCs and how the pathways connect to one another. They can speed up and slow down the team's progression through the pathways and set the pace of each meeting, which can help prevent the checklist mentality that often accompanies these types of conversation guides. A coach can challenge team members to think more deeply, which is sometimes difficult for teachers to do with their peers. He or she can bring a refreshing outside perspective and can encourage individuals to speak up where they otherwise may not be heard. A coach applying the pathways tools can help shape the culture of teams into one of true collaboration, in which members both support and challenge one another to improve student learning.

In the next chapter, we explore real-life scenarios to demonstrate how coaches can combine clarity, feedback, and support to amplify the effectiveness of their collaborative teams.

PART III

PUTTING IT ALL TOGETHER TO AMPLIFY YOUR IMPACT

CHAPTER 6

Making It Real: Coaching Scenarios

Coaching is aimed at trying to help someone learn, grow, or change.

—DOUG STONE AND SHEILA HEEN

In this chapter, we focus on application, examining two different coaching scenarios. The first scenario takes place at the fictitious A. C. Doyle Elementary, where we observe a fourth-grade team and watch as it meets to discuss the results of a language arts assessment. The setting for the second scenario is the fictitious Pratt High School, where an algebra 1 team is working to improve its instructional practices. Although these two schools are fictional, the scenarios draw on our extensive work in real schools as coaches with real teacher teams.

Our hope is that these lifelike scenarios provide concrete examples of how coaches can use clarity (the SIG); feedback (the three different coaching stances—consultant, collaborator, and coach of reflective thinking); and support (the pathways) to positively impact the overall productivity of collaborative teams in a PLC.

Each scenario is a story told in two parts.

1. Part one describes an ineffective and inefficient team meeting where, despite its best effort, the team struggles to function as a high-performing collaborative team.

2. Part two shows how a coach can intervene to produce more positive results and enhance the level of collaboration between and among the teachers on the team.

An analysis of what happened at the meeting and a series of questions for the coach to consider follows each scenario. The reader, as a coach, should think about when and how he or she might be able to intervene if coaching the team.

A. C. Doyle Elementary School

A. C. Doyle Elementary School is a small K–5 building in a modest, Midwest suburban city. The staff at Doyle has adopted the PLC philosophy as part of their continuous school-improvement process. Their principal, Mr. Watson, and key members of the school-improvement team have been trained in basic PLC concepts. In turn, they have led book studies and professional learning sessions with their teachers for several years. A local consultant has led their grade-level teams through collaboratively prioritizing standards and aligning existing curriculum to those priority standards. They have also created common formative and summative assessments for the priority standards they have identified in each unit.

Although the school has been engaged in the implementation of PLC concepts for several years, Principal Watson recognizes that many of his teams have stalled. After an initial rise in standardized assessment scores, the school has hit a plateau. The sense of urgency among teams has dwindled and achievement has remained stagnant. This year, Principal Watson convinced central office administrators to allow him to use a district instructional coach as a collaborative team coach in an effort to reignite his PLC.

Description of Inefficient, Ineffective Meeting

Today is Ms. Adler's first day as a new collaborative team coach at A. C. Doyle Elementary. The teachers at Doyle have received extensive training on the PLC process and have been meeting in collaborative teams weekly for the past three years. At Principal Watson's request, Ms. Adler will spend the day observing the fourth-grade team to get a feel for the team's current status and the next steps she will recommend for its continued growth. She and Principal Watson will debrief after collaborative team meeting time.

After Ms. Adler introduces herself and lets the team know she will mostly observe it, the team begins its meeting.

"So, what are we talking about today?" Ms. Lestrade asks.

"I'm not sure," Mrs. Holmes replies. "What do you suggest?"

Mr. Moriarty says, "We gave that text structure assessment last week. We could talk about the results."

The team agrees that this will be its topic for the day, so Ms. Adler asks for a copy of the assessment. In this district-developed test given the week prior, students had to identify the text structure of multiple text passages.

strategies

"My scores don't look so hot," Mrs. Holmes says with exasperation.

"It seems like the students in my class who circled or highlighted the text structure signal words on the test ended up with better scores," Ms. Lestrade says.

"I told my students before the test began that they needed to circle or highlight the signal words," Mr. Moriarity says. "I think my students did pretty well."

"I put my anchor chart with the signal words right at the front of the room during testing," Mrs. Holmes says. "I didn't want to direct them outright to use the strategy during the test, but I was trying to remind them of what they should be doing. I think the few students who used the anchor charts did better than the rest."

"We used that strategy in class all last week," Ms. Lestrade replies. "The students should know by now that they should use that strategy. They just don't apply the strategies we use as a whole class when they're on their own."

"It all comes down to test-taking strategies," Mr. Moriarity says. "Shouldn't we have a schoolwide anchor chart for test-taking strategies? That way there would be consistency from grade to grade, and it's more likely that the students will remember them."

Looking up from her laptop where she had been searching online for test-taking strategies, Ms. Lestrade says, "I just found some acronyms for test-taking strategies on the Teachers Pay Teachers website. This one is really cute! Let's get the whole school to use this one!"

"That's a great idea!" Ms. Lestrade exclaims. "Let's bring it up to Principal Watson at the staff meeting."

"So . . . back to the test," Mr. Moriarity says. "My students seemed to struggle with description. Recognizing description is tough because most texts include at least some form of description."

"Maybe we should change the test and start with an easier passage," Mrs. Holmes says. "If we put the easier ones first, like cause and effect, maybe students will be able to pare down to description."

"Another great idea!" Ms. Lestrade responds. "Maybe we should just take description out altogether. That way the students won't get as confused."

"Let's just plan to do that for next year," Mr. Moriarity suggests. "I almost forgot! We need to fill out the meeting summary form for Principal Watson. What are your class scores for the test?"

"Forty-five percent of my students scored proficient," Mrs. Holmes replies.

"I had 38 percent," Ms. Lestrade reports.

"And 62 percent of mine made the cut," Mr. Moriarity says. "Now the form asks us what our next steps are. It's already May 5, folks, we need to move on."

Both Ms. Lestrade and Mrs. Holmes agree. However, Ms. Adler knows this assessment draws on a priority standard that stakeholders expect students to master. She decides to take a chance and ask the team a question. "Before you move on, can you tell me how your students scored on the passages that were description?"

"I didn't grade mine that way," Ms. Lestrade answers.

"What do you mean? You want us to go through and figure out how the students scored on each different structure type? That would take forever!" Mr. Moriarity exclaims.

"Separating the scores according to targets will help us identify which students need intervention with which text structures. What if you take out your students' papers and look at that together now?" Ms. Adler asks.

As it turns out, the teachers had the students grade the tests in class and had already handed the tests back to the students. Ms. Adler is shocked that the teachers would hand back common assessments before the team had discussed the results. She feels that she has no choice but to ask the next question.

"So, what are you planning to do for the students who didn't meet the proficiency goal?" she questions.

"We really need to move on to the next unit," Mrs. Holmes responds. "We've spent too much time on this unit, and we're way behind on our scope and sequence."

"Is there a way you can incorporate this priority standard into the next unit then?" Ms. Adler asks.

"The next unit is on fiction book clubs," Mr. Moriarity says. "It will be really hard for our students to pick out text structures in fiction. We need to just move on and let the fifth-grade teachers deal with it in the fall."

With that, the morning entrance bell rings and students begin pouring through the doors.

"I have to get to my room," Mrs. Holmes states. "It will be a mess if I don't get there before the students," she adds as she runs out the door. The rest of the team packs up its belongings, eager to end the meeting.

Ms. Adler leaves the meeting realizing she has a lot of work ahead of her. She heads down the hall for the debrief meeting with Principal Watson.

"How did it go?" Principal Watson asks Ms. Adler as she walks into the office.

"Well, the teachers seem very comfortable with each other," she responds. "Can we sit down and look at the fourth-grade team's self-reflection on the SIG? I'd like to see where they placed themselves."

Ms. Adler is especially interested to see how the team rates itself on the SIG component that states, "Teacher teams use data and item analysis to manage, monitor, and adjust core instruction and intervention in the classroom." Sure enough, the team had rated this component as *implemented*.

Analysis

Ms. Adler shares the following analysis with Principal Watson about A. C. Doyle's grade 4 team.

- **The team did not develop an agenda ahead of time:** The team decided on the topic of conversation after starting the meeting. Not knowing the agenda meant that it did not have all the student work, data, or other materials it needed for a productive, collaborative team meeting.

- **The teachers talked about how their students did on the test in general terms:** They used words like "It seems like" and "I think" rather than using the actual data from the assessment to draw accurate conclusions. It was not until they remembered they are responsible for summarizing their meeting for the principal that they looked at their proficiency scores.

- **All three teachers used different test-delivery methods:** One teacher told students to highlight the signal words, another put the anchor chart at the front of the room, and the third did not mention signal words at all. This does not allow for accurate comparisons between classrooms.

- **The team got off track when it veered from assessment analysis to a conversation about test-taking strategies:** While schoolwide test-taking strategies are important, this is a topic that would be better served through a staff discussion or subcommittee focused on this specific task. Teams should spend their valuable collaborative team time in the most productive ways possible.

- **When the team went back to discussing the assessment, its first solution to low achievement was to change the test:** It is not unusual for team members to point to items or issues outside of themselves when confronted with low achievement. It is far easier to blame the test construction than it is to reflect on one's own instructional practices. In addition, the team decided to change the test for the following school year without discussing the idea with the district curriculum leader. Because this is a districtwide common assessment to measure a grade-level priority standard, consistency for all students should exist across the district. This is a basic tenet of providing students with a guaranteed and viable curriculum.

- **The team did not break down the assessment or its data into targets:** Looking at an overall proficiency percentage does not give teachers the level of detail they needs to provide students with timely and specific intervention. In fact, the team has no interest in providing students with any intervention at all, despite the low numbers of proficiency. The fact that the teachers gave students their tests back before discussing the data shows that they don't intend to use these data to inform instructional next steps.

- **Finally, the team inaccurately rates itself on the SIG:** The fact that the team rated the SIG section as implemented shows that this team either does not have an accurate understanding of what the SIG indicates, or it is not willing to honestly reflect on its PLC practices.

Questions for Consideration

As you respond to the following six questions, think about the process of using clarity, feedback, and support to identify the current reality, existing gaps, supports needed, and next steps for the team. There are not necessarily right or wrong answers to these questions, but it is important to reflect on the team-coaching process and how it might apply to the team in the scenario.

1. Which coaching stance would Ms. Adler assume if she were coaching this team (consultant, collaborator, or coach of reflective thinking)? Why would she choose that stance?

2. As the coach, what will she work on first with this team? What might give the team some easy wins?

3. How can Ms. Adler use the SIG to move this team forward?

4. What evidence can Ms. Adler use to help the team identify its true location on the SIG?

5. What feedback stems might be useful to Ms. Adler with her work with this team?

6. How can Ms. Adler use the pathways to help the team reflect on the effectiveness of its meeting?

Interventions From Coach

The fourth-grade teachers at A. C. Doyle Elementary meet in its grade-level collaborative team every Thursday morning. They receive extensive training in the PLC process and have been working collaboratively for the past three years. In an effort to grow and sustain successful collaborative teams, the district has invested in hiring PLC coaches to work with collaborative teams. Ms. Adler has been coaching the fourth-grade team for the past year and will be joining the team for today's collaborative meeting. As usual, she will meet with Principal Watson for a postmeeting debrief.

The team welcomes Ms. Adler as she walks into the team meeting. She notes that it must be Mr. Moriarty's turn to take notes for the meeting summary, as he already has his laptop open. They begin with reviewing the agenda and prepare to discuss the results of a recently administered language arts assessment. Given a week prior, the district-developed test asked students to identify the text structure of multiple text passages.

"Okay," Ms. Adler says to the group, "Since you are reviewing assessment data, we'll be using the pathway Analyzing Assessment Data. Let's start by reviewing the SMART goal."

"Our goal was that 80 percent of our students will reach 80 percent proficiency on this assessment," Mrs. Holmes says. "Let's compile our scores to see if we reached our goal."

"Thirty-eight percent of my students score proficient overall," Ms. Lestrade replies.

"Sixty-two percent of mine are proficient," Mr. Moriarity says.

"And only 45 percent of mine made the cut," Mrs. Holmes says. "We aren't even close to our goal in any of our classes."

"That adds up to 48 percent proficiency overall," Mr. Moriarity points out. "Man, that's disappointing."

"Let's look a little closer at the scores before you get too discouraged," Ms. Adler says. "What are your proficiency rates for each target?" she asks, referring to the pathways tool.

Each teacher pulls out an individual class-analysis document. As a team, the teachers compile the data onto the team-analysis form and arrive at the following numbers (see table 6.1, page 120).

Table 6.1: Team Analysis of Scores for Test on Text Structure of Multiple Passages

	Lestrade	Moriarity	Holmes	Team Average
Description	74 percent	95 percent	77 percent	82 percent
Cause and Effect	26 percent	56 percent	17 percent	33 percent
Compare and Contrast	33 percent	61 percent	47 percent	47 percent
Sequence	31 percent	59 percent	45 percent	45 percent
Problem and Solution	23 percent	40 percent	15 percent	26 percent
Average of All Targets	37 percent	62 percent	40 percent	46.6 percent

"So what patterns or trends do you see?" Ms. Adler questions, referring to the pathways tool.

"It's really strange that the students did so well on description," Mr. Moriarity points out.

"I agree," Mrs. Holmes says, shaking her head. "My students struggled identifying description during instruction because most pieces of text include some sort of description in them. My students thought all the passages were description!"

"Maybe that's why they scored so high in it," Ms. Lestrade says. "I wonder if they answered with description more often on the test so they had a better chance of identifying it correctly!"

"Maybe we should take a look at the student work to see if that is the case," Ms. Adler says. She makes a mental note to shift to the pathway Analyzing Student Work. It makes sense for them to start in the third box down, "Look at papers of students not proficient. Are there common misconceptions or mistakes? How can you correct those misconceptions or mistakes?"

The team spends the next several minutes reading through student papers, and it counts the number of times students identified a passage as descriptive. Sure enough, the team finds that some students identified multiple passages as descriptive, even though each text structure was only represented once on the assessment.

"It looks like we have some work to do on helping our students identify descriptive versus the other text structures," Ms. Lestrade says.

"Do you notice anything about the work of students who did better on this test?," Ms. Adler asks, moving to the box above on the pathways tool.

"You know, as we were looking through the tests, I noticed that the students who circled or highlighted the text structure signal words seemed to end up with better scores," Ms. Lestrade answers.

"I noticed that too," Mr. Moriarity says. "Did we all remind our students to circle the signal words like we agreed to?"

All three teachers reminded their students at the beginning of the test that they should circle the signal words to help them identify the text structure. The team had discussed and agreed on the testing conditions ahead of time so these data would be comparable among the three classes.

"Any idea why some students did it and some students didn't?" Ms. Adler asks.

"I had my anchor chart with the signal words at the front of the room so it was easy for them to remember the words," Mr. Moriarity responds.

"I didn't do that," Ms. Lestrade says.

"Me either," Mrs. Holmes says. "I wonder if the students who didn't circle the words just couldn't remember what they were."

"This could explain why Mr. Moriarty's scores were higher than the other teachers' classes," Ms. Adler says. She moves back to pathway Analyzing Assessment Data and the box that asks whether proficiency levels are higher in some classes than others. "He was the only one who put his anchor chart at the front of the room."

"Maybe we should give another short formative assessment and see if the students can list the signal words for each text structure type. That could tell us which students actually know the signal words and which don't," Mr. Moriarity says. "I'll be sure that I don't have the anchor chart at the front of the room this time so all our students are testing under the same circumstances."

"Sounds good to me. When should we give the test?" Ms. Lestrade asks.

The teachers look at their lesson plans and decide that the sooner they give the follow-up assessment, the better. They agree to give the test the next day and bring these data to their common planning period to compare. They know that the follow-up assessment data will guide their next steps for carrying this important priority standard forward into the next unit.

During the debriefing meeting with Principal Watson, Ms. Adler asks to see where the team has placed itself on the SIG. She is immediately drawn to the section that says, "Teacher teams use data and item analysis to manage, monitor, and adjust core instruction and intervention in the classroom." It rates itself as effective, which

Ms. Adler finds to be accurate. In order to move the team toward an exemplary status on the SIG, she will begin working with members on designing interventions and enrichment opportunities based on the student data.

Analysis

Ms. Adler shares the following analysis of the grade 4 team meeting with Principal Watson.

- **The team was prepared for the meeting:** Its members had identified roles and responsibilities. They also had an agenda prepared and were using it to direct the meeting.

- **The coach started with a consultant stance, directing the team to the pathways document and recommending it review the SMART goal:** She continued in the consultant stance as she asked the team to identify the proficiency rates for each target and to describe any patterns or trends members saw.

- **The coach shifted to the collaborator stance when she and the teachers began reviewing student work:** Questions like "Did you notice anything about the work of students who did better on this test?" encouraged the team to engage in dialogue and look more closely at the student work. In fact, it was this conversation that led the teachers to discover why the scores in one class were so much higher than the others.

- **The teachers agreed ahead of time on the conditions for administering the assessment:** However, these data led them to realize that one class had an advantage because the teacher changed the conditions in his classroom. The team may not have come to this realization without the coach's gentle nudging.

- **The team began to direct its own work when Mr. Moriarity suggested that it give an additional formative assessment:** Team members independently planned the kind of assessment to use, when to administer it, and when to review these data. At this time, Ms. Adler was simply acting as a coach of reflective feedback.

- **The coach and team used the pathways properly:** Ms. Adler moved between pathways according to the flow of the conversation. She was also able to identify the appropriate place to begin on each pathway, recognizing that this is not necessarily a linear process.

- **The team accurately used the SIG to plan next steps:** Through the team's self-reflection on the SIG, Ms. Adler confirmed the accuracy of its implementation level and planned next steps for moving the team forward.

Questions for Consideration

As you respond to the following five questions, think about the process of using clarity, feedback, and support to identify current reality, existing gaps, necessary supports, and next steps for the team. There are not necessarily right or wrong answers to these questions, but it is important to reflect on the team coaching process and how it might apply to the team in the scenario.

1. Which coaching stance will Ms. Adler assume to continue coaching this team (consultant, collaborator, or coach of reflective thinking)? Why would Ms. Adler choose that stance?

2. How can Ms. Adler use the SIG to move this team forward?

3. What evidence can Ms. Adler use to help the team reflect on its location on the SIG?

4. What feedback stems might be useful to Ms. Adler as she coaches this team?

5. How can the team use the pathways tool to reflect on the effectiveness of its meeting?

Pratt High School

Pratt High School begins PLC transformation with excitement and determination. In the inaugural year, the principal, instructional coach, and teacher leaders work tirelessly to train staff on the PLC philosophy and structures. As a leadership team, they attend a national PLC conference, and Pratt's staff engage in a semester-long book study centered on the three big ideas and four critical questions of PLC (DuFour et al., 2016).

Pratt's principal, Principal White, strongly advocates for the PLC process, and this positively influences Mr. Plum, the instructional coach. After learning more from the trainings, the staff also share an overall belief about the importance of PLCs, and the majority of staff members are on board to begin the work. The leadership team restructures the school's master schedule to ensure teams have time to meet during the regular school day. Department chairs assume leadership roles and do their best to facilitate the development of vertical and horizontal collaborative teams. School leadership encourages and expects that products generated from teams' collaborative meetings will be stored electronically so they are accessible to all staff and serve as examples, while having the added benefit of providing accountability.

Since the instructional coach is new to the PLC process, Mr. Plum values his role as learner alongside teachers. Both the coach and the principal know monitoring implementation is critical to sustaining the PLC process. However, it is still vague to both Mr. Plum and Principal White how they will actualize this, so they begin with supporting staff the best they can. Mr. Plum shifts his focus from individual teacher support toward working alongside the collaborative teams. As a result, Mr. Plum adjusts his schedule to participate in team meetings as much as possible. While in these meetings, Mr. Plum helps in various ways. Sometimes that means he observes, interjecting questions when the teams seem to stray, and at other times it means he facilitates the best he can. In reality, he's just steps ahead of the teams in his own PLC knowledge. Since Principal White can't attend all team meetings, she relies on monthly debriefs in which Mr. Plum updates her with his perceptions of how the collaborative work is progressing across the school.

When the school's leadership team convenes in March to begin planning for the following year, department chairs share a concerning trend that teams are growing frustrated and feel stuck with the PLC process. The department chairs state that they feel inadequate to help teams determine next steps, as those steps are unclear. Mr. Plum echoes that he notices this trend and reiterates his low efficacy and the belief that he is letting down the teams.

The following scenarios highlight two different responses that occur as a result of the end-of-year leadership meeting.

Description of Inefficient, Ineffective Meeting

Principal White shares that perhaps time off over the summer will help, and teams will come back ready to go and be able to problem solve the rough spots they encounter in their meetings. The leadership team also agrees that it has offered substantial training and that teams have done their best to apply learning over the past year.

Three weeks into the new school year, Mr. Plum is hopeful as he steps into the room to observe the algebra 1 team for the first time. "What are we working on today?" Mr. Plum asks as he sits down to join the algebra team.

While Mr. Mustard pulls up the electronic document on the screen in front of the group, Mrs. Peacock starts sharing, "We want to show you something. When we got back together at the beginning of the school year we were talking about how frustrated we were at the end of last year. We think this work could be helpful to our team, but the more we meet, the more we tend to feel directionless. So, look at what we have done."

"In our online document, we have built an agenda that includes our norms, collective commitments, and some places to document our progress with the four critical questions of a PLC. We figured this might help keep us focused and on track," Miss Scarlet explains.

"Last week we determined essential learning in the upcoming linear functions and equations unit. Today, we think it would be important to develop an end-of-unit common assessment. Our concern is that it was really difficult to come to consensus on what is essential," Mr. Mustard says. "I am more than a little worried about how today's planning session will play out."

"Yes, it seems we all have different ideas, and at times it feels we lack clarity on next steps and processes that would help us through our dissonance," Mr. Green responds.

"I agree. We are doing the best we can, but there are lots of different perspectives on our mathematics team. I'm anxious that coming up with a common assessment we all agree on is going to be nearly impossible," Miss Scarlet says.

Mr. Green interjects, "I know we need to do that, and we said we would try to do it. But I have developed my assessments that have worked for me. I'm good with my way. I gave my assessments last year and got good results. So, I'm wondering whether I need to even opt into this conversation."

"Yes, but if we don't have a common assessment, how will we measure if all our students have learned the material?" Mr. Mustard asks.

"And more important, there is an expectation that we bring common assessment data to this table and have conversations about it. That's an expectation from Mrs. White and the leadership team," Mrs. Peacock says.

"Quite frankly, I don't care what data we bring to the table. I know what my data tell me about what I'm doing in my classroom. I know we agreed to work together, but I'm really struggling because what you are doing in your classroom isn't going to impact me. My students are different and so is my classroom. I don't see why I have to participate. And we spent all this time last year trying to determine what was essential and develop common assessments, but when we got stuck we would just spin and spin. I am seeing that trend play out again early this year too. This is so frustrating," Mr. Green says. "If there was a better way with different dynamics and we had more direction, I might feel different. We are all still fairly new to this process, and not much has changed since last year."

"Wow, sounds like you are unhappy," Mr. Plum says.

"No, I'm really just frustrated. The amount of time we spend in directionless conversations is truly impacting everything related to my teaching. I know we have an agenda we have to fill out, but our purpose is not any clearer. So, if you don't mind, I'll stay in the room and plan on my own, but will not join the conversation," Mr. Green says as he moved to a separate table away from the group.

"Well, I think we are supposed to do this together, right? It's an all-school initiative. Can we just have the conversation together?" Mr. Plum asks.

"I suppose," Mr. Green says. "I don't want to stand in the way of the group or be 'that guy,'" he says as he held his hands in air quotes, "but you need to know where I stand!"

Mr. Plum attempts to pull the group together and asks, "Okay, Mr. Green, can you pull up your assessments you've used and show us? Maybe we can use them as a starting point."

"Well, before you share, look at mine. I've been teaching for twenty years, and I know I have the best assessment to use," Mr. Mustard says. "Here, let me pull the electronic copy up so you can see it."

As the team reviews what Mr. Mustard shares, Miss Scarlet responds, "Okay. You want me to use this, I can do that. I like it. It is way better than what I have. I don't have the years of experience in teaching that you have."

"No problem, I've got this down, and I'll give you all the materials I've used along the way," Mr. Mustard says.

"I don't know. We had all better get on the same page," Mrs. Peacock asserts. "Isn't this about students having common outcomes, expectations, and high levels of learning in all our classrooms—not just each of us individually teaching? You may both have it right [*motioning to Mr. Green and Mr. Mustard*], but even so, we'd better do this together. I don't like how Mr. Green removed himself from the group earlier, nor how Miss Scarlet willingly goes along with everything Mr. Mustard says."

Mr. Plum attempts once again to refocus the group. "Everyone, I'd ask that we all pause for a moment. When I look at your agenda, I notice you include the seven norms of collaboration from Garmston and Wellman [2016]: (1) promoting a spirit of inquiry, (2) pausing, (3) paraphrasing, (4) probing for specificity, (5) putting ideas on the table, (6) paying attention to self and others, and (7) presuming positive intentions [AllThingsPLC, n.d.]. Why don't we take time to look over these before we go any further?"

The team members, complying with this request, all look at the screen showing the seven norms of collaboration they had agreed to implement in a previous meeting.

"While I appreciate these norms and agree with them, this continuous spin is polarizing our team. Norms can only go so far, and they won't fix this lack of clarity we are feeling. I am not even sure we know what our next steps should be. I may be newer to teaching, but I am no less frustrated than any of you," Miss Scarlet says with an exasperated sigh. "There has to be a better way. When we all started the PLC work last year we were really pumped. So much seems to have changed between then and now."

"This is just turning into every other planning session. Last week, we couldn't agree on what students should learn in the function and equations unit. Heck, I'm not even sure I want to participate," Mr. Green states matter-of-factly.

"Well, here we are again disagreeing on our purpose, how to work together, and ultimately our task at hand today of developing a common assessment," Mr. Mustard adds.

"You know, let's pull out the *Learning by Doing* book [DuFour et al., 2016] we studied last year. The text might have some ideas that we just haven't thought through, or at least are worth revisiting. I think this uneasy feeling that we are experiencing is fairly common," Mr. Plum offers as he begins paging through his copy of the book looking for information on common assessments.

"How will we ever get to the work if we always have to go back to the book? We are grab bagging," Mr. Mustard says.

"See, what a waste of time," Mr. Green exclaims. "Fine, I cannot give this mess any more time. Mr. Mustard, please send me the assessment you shared. I'll implement it if you all feel it will help move the team forward. I have other work to tend to that is a better use of my time right now." Mr. Green collects his materials and leaves the meeting.

"Well, that was dramatic! Can the four of us agree to work a bit longer and look at the assessment to see if it matches the essentials we determined last week?" Mrs. Peacock asks. "You know, using equations to graph lines and determine slope?"

Mr. Mustard and Miss Scarlet shake their heads in unison and disbelief. Mr. Mustard begins reviewing the assessment and, after a brief review, shares, "This assessment has possibilities but doesn't completely align to using equations to graph lines or determining slope. I'm not sure if the level of proficiency is high enough."

"I agree," Miss Scarlet concurs.

"I'm good with this. For goodness sake, time is running out! There are at least a few questions that hit on the essentials we agreed our students should know," Mrs. Peacock says.

"I just disagree. These questions are just not at a high enough level for the students in my classroom," Mr. Mustard says.

Mr. Plum says, "I think we need to go back to *Learning by Doing* by DuFour and his coauthors. There is good information in here, and it might help us. We must consider some of the ideas when we meet again, but right now we have only three minutes left before your students return. Let's tie this up. I think we have a few questions from the common assessment that might be a starting point. Also, we need to keep everyone in the room for planning."

The team meeting adjourns in a quick manner.

The following day, Mr. Plum and Principal White meet to debrief the algebra team meeting.

"How was yesterday's meeting with the algebra team?" Principal White asks.

Mr. Plum responds, "The meeting was tough. It was apparent that the team was not focused and the teachers were grasping for answers. I completely understand where they are at, because, honestly, I feel the same way."

"You are feeling frustrated. I sense that. What do you suggest?" Principal White asks.

"We need to rethink our implementation plan and reboot."

Analysis

Mr. Plum shares the following analysis with Principal White after the first Pratt High algebra 1 team meeting.

- **The principal is correct to establish a leadership team:** The leadership team—a guiding coalition composed of administration, the instructional coach, and teacher leaders—makes implementing PLCs more effective because of its diverse leadership.

- **The school lacks a long-range implementation plan that would ensure clear action steps to apply the learning:** Planning for common training and setting some tight expectations is a good first step. However, training combined with the implied message of, "Go forth and collaborate!" is a misstep. Continued training does not always assure high-quality implementation.

- **Within the PLC process, role definition has yet to occur:** The instructional coach has noble intentions and would benefit from a clearly defined role within aligned PLC structures. Defining what is tight and what is loose is critical for both the staff who are new to the PLC process and the coach. Clarity is present when each stakeholder group has a defined role within the PLC structure and clear next steps.

- **The instructional coach's role is vague:** Being intentional is much different than being willing to help. The coach's lack of clarity regarding PLCs combined with being expected to support and monitor the progress of teams without a defined and transparent process is a setup for failure.

- **The team's frustration leads to more of the status quo:** Members decided to push forward with the status quo hoping the team's collaborative practice would improve. Hope is *not* a strategy. The principal and instructional coach failed to realize that team members need intentional, ongoing support to improve. Without clear feedback connected to one of the critical questions of learning or a big idea, team members were left to approximate their next steps.

- **The team clarifies why PLC transformation and work are important; however, it stops there:** Lack of clarity on why, how, and what to implement hampered the faculty as the first year folded into the next. Teachers started out knowing the PLC process and that collaborative work can help improve outcomes for students, but they started to become directionless, which led to conflict and potentially jeopardized implementation.

- **Implementation is hampered because the school lacks a clear plan to implement:** The school recognized the instructional coach could be a valuable asset to help move teams forward. A transparent schoolwide support and monitoring plan would have helped the efficacy of both the coach and school teams.

- **The team's lack of clarity hinders the process:** Without clarity, the team could not identify where to start nor determine next steps. They were approximating and guessing what to do next. When expectations combined with an absence of clarity around processes and long-term plans, the team gravitated toward a state of compliance when members did not see their collaborative practice improving.

Questions for Consideration

As you respond to the following three questions, think about the process of using clarity, feedback, and support to identify current reality, necessary support, and next steps for the team. There are not necessarily right or wrong answers to these questions, but it is important to reflect on the team-coaching process and how it might apply to the team in the scenario.

Mr. Plum reflects on Pratt High's PLC implementation and the impact specifically on the algebra 1 team, considering the following three questions. (Any coach can use these questions when he or she encounters a team like the algebra 1 team.)

1. Pratt High's leadership assumes that ongoing training alone focused on PLCs will strengthen the schools collaborative teams. How does this assumption impact the mathematics team? Thinking forward to the school's continuous training related to the PLC process, what other support is the school providing to teacher teams?

2. Mr. Plum helps collaborative teams the best he can. However, how might clear outcomes for teams' success help clarify a purposeful role in collaborative planning? How can the school leadership team define success and identify the structures to support teams?

3. The mathematics team grew frustrated at Pratt High, leading to conflict due to a lack of progress and inability to determine next steps. In what ways might this frustration and conflict have been avoided or lessened? Moving forward, what can Mr. Plum remember from this scenario to help him avoid a similar outcome?

Interventions From Coach

As Pratt High School teachers return in the fall, Principal White and Mr. Plum share their thoughts with staff about the need to clarify collaborative teamwork. They share a plan they developed with the leadership team over the summer. They comment that this year they want to be more intentional in their monitoring of and support for teams. To set the stage, they use data from prior year team observations as well as feedback data they received from department chairs.

As a result, Principal White and Mr. Plum facilitate the process, with the entire staff, to develop a SIG and the progression of indicators tied to the essential elements of PLC. On completion, the clarity the SIG provided produces a road map that Pratt teams can follow to become high-functioning teams. This opportunity to define the specific work of PLCs is a grounding activity for the entire staff. The school reflects together while developing the SIG to create clarity for its year two PLC work. Equally important, the SIG reminds teams in a concrete way of the common vocabulary aligned to PLC implementation.

After the team develops the SIG, Mr. Plum leads team members through a process in which the team uses artifacts and products from its prior year's team meetings to self-assess and determine the team's current reality in relation to the indicators on the SIG. Each team creates an action plan connected to the anchors and indicators using language from the SIG. Mr. Plum follows this with a process in which each team creates its own plan to meet the goal. In their plan, team members establish timelines and dates when they want Principal White or Mr. Plum to meet with them, provide feedback on their progress, and work with them to identify their next steps.

Mr. Plum is looking forward to today's scheduled progress-monitoring check-in with the four teachers on the algebra team regarding the long-term goal the team establishes.

"Hello everyone. I'm excited to join you today. I reviewed your online action plan last night and looked over the goal you set. I can tell you care about this work," Mr. Plum says. "Just to double-check so that I am clear: the goal you identified is to have an agreed-on timeline for assessments. Does this sound correct?"

"Yes. That is our focus," Mr. Mustard says.

"Great! Before we go any further, I want to take a few minutes and lay out the process for today's conversation," Mr. Plum says. "The outcome of our time together is to identify successes and next steps as we continue to move forward in this collaborative work. Remember, we will use the SIG as a reference point for this check-in. I also want to let you know that as I facilitate this conversation with all school teams, the information that surfaces will help us identify emerging trends and themes that will help Mrs. White, the leadership team, and me to support and plan for professional learning at Pratt. So, I will record your ideas." Mr. Plum opens his notebook to begin writing.

"Are we good to start?" Mr. Plum asks.

The team members nod their heads.

"Okay, the protocol we will use for this conversation might feel very structured, but this will help us stay on track and highlight specific information to help your team and our school with implementation of the PLC process. Please share what progress you have made toward your goal, and share any products you feel are important. Next, we will celebrate successes, talk about where you might be stuck, and I'll do my best to offer you some feedback. As we conclude, you can either keep going on your current plan or make adjustments based on the feedback. Sound good? What questions do you have?" Mr. Plum asks.

The group responds in unison, "We're good."

"Great. To help me understand the context, share with me why you chose this particular goal," Mr. Plum says.

"Well, we looked at the indicators on the SIG," Mrs. Peacock says, "and realized that we were only giving students common summative assessments, and not common formative assessments."

"We were missing some ways to monitor student progress prior to the end of our units," Miss Scarlet says.

"Although the SIG is helping us see the bigger picture of PLC implementation and our next steps, one of our biggest insights came when we looked at sections under the pathway Creating Common Formative Assessments," Mr. Mustard says. "Two of the pathway's questions were, 'What targets will you address on this CFA?' and 'What targets from previous instruction do you need to reassess?' These questions caused us to review our summative assessments. We realized that many of the test questions didn't align to what we determined was essential for our students to know."

"I agree. What was really noticeable was that we didn't have a long-term assessment plan," Mrs. Peacock says. "We spent a ton of time last year determining what was essential for our students to master, only to find out we were lacking ongoing ways to identify if they were even learning."

"So, based on all of this, how is your progress toward the goal you set?" Mr. Plum asks.

"Let me pull up our electronic documents to show you what we've come up with," Mr. Mustard says as he motions to the screen. "Here is our assessment timeline for our last unit on linear functions and equations."

"Notice that we have developed a common summative assessment, and what's really cool is that we were purposeful in trying to make sure that questions on the assessment matched what we said were essential for kids to know," Miss Scarlet says. "You also see that we planned a few common formative assessments in the middle of the unit to ensure students are on the right track to mastery. As a newer teacher, this really provides me a clearer direction than I had in the past."

Mrs. Peacock jumps in, "For example, on the summative assessment, we asked students to graph a line based on an equation that was given to them. Also, students had to demonstrate that they can write an equation based on a line given to them. The common formative assessments we gave mid-unit checked students' understanding around the different parts of an equation."

"So, it sounds like you are feeling like you've made progress toward your goal," Mr. Plum says. He goes on to ask, "Is your team thinking this continues to be the 'right' goal?"

"I'm not sure. I know it feels right, and as we looked at the SIG, we all agreed this was the correct move for us," Mr. Green answers.

"I agree. However, when we shared our end-of-unit assessment results with each other, I kept wondering if we had missed the mark. Remember, we all agreed that our results weren't stellar," Miss Scarlet comments.

"That's right. So, is this the right goal?" Mr. Green questions, looking around the table.

"Well, before you determine that, tell me more about how you developed your timeline," Mr. Plum says.

"What you see is our finished time line," Miss Scarlet says, referring to the online document. "On the calendar, we determined key dates to administer assessments. A few days before giving the assessment, we planned and wrote the questions together, identified the proficiency levels, and made sure they matched to the essential learnings for the unit."

"It's important that you are considering the use of both formative and summative assessments. This is a solid practice, and you are understanding how having check-ins throughout a unit is important to monitoring student learning. Since you didn't get the results you expected on the end-of-unit assessment, and knowing that you developed each assessment a couple of days in advance of administering them, how might creating your assessment timeline as well as the common assessments prior to teaching the unit impact student learning and change your results?" Mr. Plum asks.

"Oh, that's interesting," Mr. Green says. "Your questions make me think about when we created these assessments. I remembering thinking I haven't taught to the level of the assessment we just created."

"I agree. I felt the same way," Mrs. Peacock says.

"Mr. Plum, as I reflect on your question, I think if we would have created the time-line and all the assessments before teaching the unit, it definitely would have changed my instructional practices from the beginning of the unit," Mr. Mustard says.

"You are right. It would have determined proficiency before we started teaching the unit," Mr. Green says.

"Now I'm also thinking that we may have started teaching with different expectations in mind," Miss Scarlet shares. "And, it would be awesome if we determined this prior."

"So, you all feel that if you would have put together your assessment timeline as part of your unit planning and determined the content of your assessments up front, you would have different student results," Mr. Plum says.

Everyone nods.

"What's your next step?" Mr. Plum asks. "What support do you need from me?"

"We need to take time to create our assessment timeline now for the unit that starts in two weeks. We also need to create our formative and summative assessments ahead of our instruction so we can ensure we all are on the same page. Does that sound right?" Mr. Mustard questions.

"Yes. And, our last timeline was out of sync, and now we can fix that," Mrs. Peacock echoes. "As far as supports for us, I'm not sure. What do you suggest, Mr. Plum?"

Mr. Plum says, "Would it help if I work side by side with the team as you design a common formative assessment using a test-planning blueprint?"

"That would be great!" Mrs. Peacock says. "I remember we read about the test-planning blueprint last year, we just may not have been ready to put it into context. Our next unit on quadratic equations starts in two weeks. If we can schedule a time with you next week to design that assessment blueprint, then we can teach the unit having planned for assessment in advance."

Mr. Plum says, "I am available during your planning time next Wednesday. Will that work for the team?"

"That's a date," the group responds.

"One last thing." Mr. Mustard says. "When I think about a timeline for this emerging goal, it would be great if you could check in with us when we share our end-of-unit assessment results. We can make adjustments from there and hopefully we'll see an impact of this plan on student learning."

"Okay, great! Go ahead and pull up your action plan and add this as your next goal," Mr. Plum says. "Just as you developed in your last plan, it will be important for the team to identify how you will know you have been successful and what artifacts and products you will generate to show it. Also, remember to add the date that I can join you for sharing the end-of-unit results. This will help me know when to check back in with the team."

The planning session ends. Later, in a debrief conversation between Mr. Plum and Principal White, Mr. Plum says, "The algebra team made progress on its goal of developing an assessment timeline for its last unit. The team thought an important next step would be to develop a timeline and common assessments prior to teaching the next unit. I have scheduled time to meet with the team next week to support it through this conversation. I will also cycle back to talk about student outcomes."

Analysis

Mr. Plum shares the following analysis with Principal White about the second Pratt High team meeting.

- **The team used the SIG, pathways tool, and goal setting to have student-centered conversations:** Using the tools led to decreased conflict. As a team, teachers felt they were moving forward with implementation.

- **The team made progress based on the goals it set:** The coach facilitated the progress when he engaged in a conversation utilizing data that affirmed the team's progress. The coach chose to take a collaborator stance because the team was making progress toward its goal. Employing a collaborator stance, the coach used verbiage that acknowledged the team's success and provided a scaffold or step to the desired goal.

- **The team clarified next steps:** The team set a long-term goal for improvement based on the SIG and recognized the importance of the pathways tool to support next steps. Specifically, the team considered questions from the pathways tool.

  - What targets will you address on the common formative assessment?

  - What targets from previous instruction will you need to reassess?

- **The team demonstrated that collaboration works:** The progress-monitoring session the algebra 1 team held with the coach provided evidence that the principal and coach's strategic decision to include faculty in the development of the SIG had empowered the team, and its members garnered a greater sense of clarity, ownership, and direction.

- **The school has a process in place to implement the PLC process:** By generating a process for a cycle of improvement whereby each team uses the SIG to set long-terms goals, an action plan, and a resulting timeline, the school provided purpose and direction for the work of teams across the school. This helped the team prioritize next steps to improve its collaborative practice. The presence of a common goal unified the team so that *we* became more important than *me*.

- **The coach monitored the team's progress:** The coach helped generate schoolwide themes for learning because he monitored the team's SIG-based action plans. The coach's consistent check-in with the principal elevated monitoring to the leadership level.

- **The coach took a collaborator stance:** The coach gave the team an opportunity to talk about its success and share artifacts that supported its progress. He also offered a suggestion that propelled the team to a deeper level of understanding.

- **The team embraced working with a coach:** As the team set a goal and created an action plan connected to the SIG, the coach's role became more purposeful because there was a plan to which to anchor.

Questions to Consider

As you respond to the following three questions, think about the process of using clarity, feedback, and support to identify current reality, necessary support, and next steps for the team. There are not necessarily right or wrong answers to these questions, but it is important to reflect on the team-coaching process and how it might apply to the team in the scenario.

As Mr. Plum reflects on Pratt's PLC implementation and the impact specifically on the algebra 1 team, he considers the three following questions. (Coaches can take time to reflect on and discuss these questions with their team to deepen each team member's individual understanding and strengthen PLC implementation for the school.)

1. As Pratt begins its second year of PLC implementation, the leadership team makes an important decision to engage the entire staff in the creation of a SIG. Why is this decision foundational to the success of PLC implementation, and how does it influence the algebra 1 team's ownership of direction and next steps? Thinking forward, what can the team consider to influence ownership of direction and next steps?

2. Pratt's algebra team developed an action plan and timeline for monitoring progress that provided purpose and direction. What does Mr. Plum notice about the intentionality of the team's planning that led to the development of its next steps? How might this scenario alter the intentionality related to how Mr. Plum will support the team to increase effectiveness?

3. Mr. Plum entered the collaborative team meeting with a defined role to support the team's long-term plan. This allowed him to focus on the conversation and provide feedback as a collaborator. He asks himself, "What do I notice about myself and my guidance on the algebra 1 team's direction?" In regard to PLC implementation, what should the school remember as the team defined Mr. Plum's role as coach?

Conclusion

When coaching collaborative teams around improving PLC practices, the focus is not on content but on developing the capacity of teachers to deliver a guaranteed and viable curriculum, design valid and reliable assessments, and develop effective intervention programs, all while sharing and reflecting on the effectiveness of their instructional practice through the lens of student learning. All these ideas increase student achievement and apply to any content area.

Coaches of collaborative teams focus their time and energy on helping teams of teachers implement the three big ideas and answer the four critical questions of a PLC. The overarching goal is to improve a team's ability to collaborate effectively. Through the process of collaborating, teachers understand that they improve their instructional practice as well. Teachers will deepen their content knowledge and sharpen their pedagogy as a natural outcome of the collaborative process.

The context of coaching is fluid. Management training expert Ken Blanchard and consulting expert Don Shula (2001) argue that, "As a coach, you need to help those around you to become flexible. From today, ensure that you're flexible enough to adapt to new realities and help others do the same" (p. 53). Coaches are most effective when they deliver the right kind of support, at the right time, in the right context.

AFTERWORD

The fundamental reason for seeking team coaching is to create high performing teams—teams that perform as more than the sum of their parts.

—RICHARD BOSTON

We are convinced that coaching collaborative teams around improving their PLC practice represents the best way to improve our schools. The rapidly increasing pace of social change, development of new technologies, and ubiquitous availability of information will continue to impact our schools.

Tomorrow's educational environment will likely be more complex, uncertain, and ambiguous than today's, but we believe schools that embrace PLCs, and the importance of collaborative teams within those PLCs, will be uniquely positioned to respond to future developments in education.

As change accelerates and education becomes more complicated, the need for collaboration will grow. As the need for collaboration grows, so too, will the importance of highly effective collaborative teams. If the goal is to ensure high levels of collaboration in our schools, and if we believe that given enough time and support all teams can collaborate at high levels, what might team coaching look like in ten years? What trends will likely influence the future of coaching, and what direction will coaching need to take to keep up with those trends?

In the future, teachers will work simultaneously in both synchronous and asynchronous settings. Virtual teaming will become even more commonplace. Innovations like flipped classrooms and assistive technologies (such as bug-in-ear coaching) will continue to attract a lot of attention. No one can say for certain how technology will affect teaching and learning, but certainly coaches and collaborative teams will play an important role in the successful implementation of these promising innovations.

The continued development of mobile devices promises to give teachers, parents, and students greater access to data, and as the expectation that information be instantaneously available becomes the norm, teachers will need the help of coaches to facilitate the kind of data conversations that enable teams to turn data around quickly.

School systems are embracing social media as a vehicle for promoting the development of collaboration. New ways of delivering professional development and the role of social networking will become more influential as Baby Boomers retire and Millennials take their place. Many organizations are investing in social-collaboration tools to better engage employees and foster more robust coaching cultures. Tools like document sharing, discussion forums, and blogs are growing in popularity (Wentworth & Lombardi, 2014). We do not foresee any of these developments going away, and teams will require the support of coaches to navigate these new environments.

Adaptive learning, sometimes called adaptive teaching, allows individuals to learn new information at their own pace. While the use of e-learning strategies makes training more accessible, an advantage for younger generations of teachers who value flexibility, e-learning suffers from some of the same limitations as more traditional forms of professional development. According to Richard Boston (LeaderSpace, 2014), without coaching it doesn't matter where or how teachers learn new information because "people fail to implement much of what they've learned whether they learn it remotely or in a classroom." Coaching is the best way to ensure that new instructional strategies transfer from the workshop to the classroom and ultimately become part of a teacher's instructional practice.

The use of technology has the potential to promote higher levels of engagement, but without the coaching of teachers in collaborative teams, technology can also become just another way of delivering the same old traditional models of professional development, which, according to Wentworth and Lombardi (2014), have done little "to improve engagement and performance."

Another set of questions revolves around the competencies necessary for team coaching. Are they the same as those necessary for instructional coaching? If the primary structure of coaching shifts from one-to-one to one-to-many relationships, how will schools and districts equip the existing cadre of instructional coaches to be effective team coaches?

The International Coach Federation (ICF) recognizes eleven core coaching competencies, and all of them apply equally to coaching individuals or teams. (Visit the ICF website [coachfederation.org] to read more about the competencies.) What is important to understand is that the traditional instructional coaching models—those that focus on working with individual teachers—and coaching frameworks that are more attentive to the needs of collaborative teams share the same goal: to help teachers improve their practice in ways that lead to higher and higher levels of student learning.

Beyond that common goal, all coaching shares some other similarities. Whether working with either individual teachers or teams of teachers, coaches need to:

- Understand adult learning theory

- Possess solid facilitation skills

- Embrace the notion that coaching can improve a teacher's practice

In either an individual or team setting, everyone involved benefits when school leaders establish clear roles and responsibilities for the coach, principal, and teachers. Coaches will have the greatest impact when teams see them as members of the guiding coalition or part of the building leadership team (which would provide credibility for the coach's role) but not as a member of the administrative team (which would make it harder to develop trust).

It is clear from both research and practice that coaches are not effective as part of the formal teacher-evaluation process: "Having the same person serve as both coach and evaluator can undercut the trusting relationships needed between coaches and teachers and may result in superficial or infrequent feedback" (Kraft et al., 2017, p. 30).

Without a trusting relationship, "no matter the expertise or enthusiasm of a coach, coaching is unlikely to impact instructional practice" (Kraft et al., 2017, p. 31). Coaches are most successful helping teachers improve their practice when their work stems from inquiry and support rather than judgment or the assessment of teacher effectiveness.

One final emerging trend that is impacting coaching and professional development is the shift from individuals to teams as the primary focus of school improvement. This shift is placing a premium on development of high-performing collaborative teams. Reflecting on his experience as a principal in Jefferson County, Colorado, Ian Stone acknowledged that, "We have done lots of work at the school level, and lots of work at the individual teacher level, but very little work has been done at the team level" (I. Stone, personal communication, November, 2017).

Boston (LeaderSpace, 2014) agrees and reports that "organizations and leaders are increasingly seeing the team as the unit of performance—not the individual." Boston (2014) goes on to say that "investing in individual training [coaching] is a smaller investment with disproportionately smaller yields." He continues, "Honing the whole team means investing more for significantly greater rewards."

A collaborative culture is best supported by a coaching culture. Done well, coaching collaborative teams leads to the creation of a coaching culture. Anne Graham (as cited in Forbes Coaches Council, 2016) argues:

> The days of sitting in three-day courses designed to fix skill deficiencies are done. Time-consuming weekly one-on-one meetings to coach and coax are done. The new model for high performance is to implement hands-on, learn/do programs related to specific business [school improvement] outcomes, where teams receive on the job training and mentoring from an expert, and hold themselves accountable to perform at a high level.

Graham is describing a coaching culture.

According to the Forbes Coaches Council (2016), a coaching culture "emphasizes training, regular feedback, and opportunities for growth" and "creates a more engaged and energized workforce." Karen Williams (2011) defines a coaching culture as one where "there is a culture of collaboration and facilitation among staff and managers [principals]." Others in the field of coaching say that a coaching culture will likely have "higher levels of motivation and commitment to the organization" (Williams, 2011) and argue that "if you are going to retain and develop talent, it has to be more than coaching; it has be to be a whole coaching culture" (Williams & Wright, 2007, p. 64). Larry Boyer (as cited in Forbes Coaches Council, 2016) says the key to creating a coaching culture is "to educate teams about what coaching is and then have them do it—coach each other." The successful organization of the future will consciously create a coaching culture to support collaborative teams as the primary unit of school improvement.

With the emergence of PLCs, the importance of highly effective collaborative teams has never been more evident. In this book, we explore the importance of coaching and collaboration as both separate and integrated concepts. We advocate for a shift in coaching priorities away from individual teachers towards collaborative teams and articulated a compelling argument for coaching collaborative teams around improving their PLC practices. Finally, we describe a coaching framework anchored in the cornerstones of clarity, feedback, and support.

We believe coaching collaborative teams in PLCs is the next generation of best practice in the coaching discipline. Hopefully, these ideas have caused you to reflect on your school's current coaching practices.

REFERENCES AND RESOURCES

Ainsworth, L. (2003). *"Unwrapping" the standards: A simple process to make standards manageable.* Denver, CO: Advanced Learning Press.

Ainsworth, L. (2004). *Power standards: Identifying the standards that matter most.* Englewood, CO: Advanced Learning Press.

AllThingsPLC. (n.d.). *7 norms of collaboration.* Accessed at www.allthingsplc.info /files/uploads/7-norms-of-collaboration-poster.pdf on September 12, 2017.

Annenberg Institute for School Reform. (2004). *Professional development strategies: Professional learning communities/instructional coaching.* Providence, RI: Author.

Apple. (2017). *Apple beta software program: Frequently asked questions.* Accessed at https://beta.apple.com/sp/betaprogram/faq on October 22, 2017.

Bailey, K., & Jakicic, C. (2012). *Common formative assessment: A toolkit for Professional Learning Communities at Work.* Bloomington, IN: Solution Tree Press.

Barber, M., Chijioke, C., & Mourshed, M. (2010). *How the world's most improved school systems keep getting better.* London: McKinsey.

Barr, K., Simmons, B., & Zarrow, J. (2003, April 21–25). *School coaching in context: A case study in capacity building.* Paper presented at the annual meeting of the American Educational Research Association, Chicago.

Basileo, L. D. (2016). *Did you know? Your school's PLCs have a major impact.* West Palm Beach, FL: Learning Sciences International.

Bickel, D. D., Bernstein-Danis, T., & Matsumura, L. C. (2015). Clear goals, clear results: Content-focused routines support learning for everyone—including coaches. *Journal of Staff Development, 36*(1), 34–39.

Blanchard, K., & Shula, D. (2001). *The little book of coaching: Motivating people to be winners.* New York: HarperBusiness.

Boatright, B., & Gallucci, C. (2008). Coaching for instructional improvement: Themes in research and practice. *Washington State Kappan*, *2*(1), 3–5.

BrainyQuote. (n.d.). *Henry Kissinger quotes.* Accessed at www.brainyquote.com /quotes/quotes/h/henrykissi153473.html on April 8, 2017.

Brasel, J., Garner, B., Kane, B., & Horn, I. (2015). Getting to the why and how. *Educational Leadership*, *73*(3). Accessed at www.ascd.org/publications /educational-leadership/nov15/vol73/num03/Getting-to-the-Why-and-How.aspx on November 29, 2015.

Bridges, W. (1991). *Managing transitions: Making the most of change.* Reading, MA: Addison-Wesley.

Briggs, T. (2013). *Developing future leaders with mentoring and coaching.* Accessed at www.td.org/Publications/Blogs/Management-Blog/2013/07/Developing-Future -Leaders-with-Mentoring-and-Coaching on November 9, 2017.

Buffum, A., Mattos, M., & Weber, C. (2010). *Pyramid response to intervention: RTI, professional learning communities, and how to respond when kids don't learn.* Bloomington, IN. Solution Tree Press.

Carroll, T. (2009). The next generation of learning teams. *Phi Delta Kappan*, *91*(2), 8–13.

Conzemius, A. E., & O'Neill, J. (2014). *The handbook for SMART school teams: Revitalizing best practices for collaboration* (2nd ed.). Bloomington, IN: Solution Tree Press.

Cornett, J., & Knight, J. (2009). Research on coaching. In J. Knight (Ed.), *Coaching: Approaches and perspectives* (pp. 192–216). Thousand Oaks, CA: Corwin Press.

Crooks, T. J. (1988). The impact of classroom evaluation practices on students. *Review of Educational Research*, *58*(4), 438–481. Thousand Oaks, CA: Sage.

Costa, A. L., & Kallick, B. (2008). *Learning and leading with habits of mind: 16 essential characteristics for success.* Alexandria, VA: Association for Supervision and Curriculum Development.

Cuban, L. (2010, June 8). *The difference between "complicated" and "complex" matters* [Blog post]. Accessed at https://larrycuban.wordpress.com/2010/06/08/the -difference-between-complicated-and-complex-matters on November 28, 2016.

Datnow, A., & Park, V. (2015). Five (good) ways to talk about data. *Educational Leadership, 73*(3), 10–15. Accessed at www.ascd.org/publications/educational -leadership/nov15/vol73/num03/Five-(Good)-Ways-to-Talk-About-Data.aspx on November 20, 2016.

Day, I. (2016). *What is the future of coaching?* Accessed at www.linkedin.com/pulse /what-future-coaching-ian-day? on November 4, 2017.

Delehant, A. M. (2006). *Making meetings work: How to get started, get going, and getting it done.* Thousand Oakes, CA: Corwin Press.

Desimone, L. M., & Pak, K. (2017). Instructional coaching as high-quality professional development. *Theory Into Practice, 56*(1), 3–12.

Di Stefano, G., Gino, F., Pisano, G., & Staats, B. (2014). *Learning by thinking: How reflection improves performance* (HBS Working Paper No. 14–093). Accessed at http://hbswk.hbs.edu/item/learning-by-thinking-how-reflection-improves -performance on July 12, 2017.

DuFour, R. (2015a). *In praise of American educators: And how they can become even better.* Bloomington, IN: Solution Tree Press.

DuFour, R. (2015b, May 8). *In praise of American educators: And how they can get even better.* Speech presented at the Summit on Professional Learning Communities at Work, Phoenix, AZ.

DuFour, R., DuFour, R., Eaker, R., Many, T. W., & Mattos, M. (2016). *Learning by doing: A handbook for Professional Learning Communities at Work* (3rd ed.). Bloomington, IN: Solution Tree Press.

DuFour, R., & Eaker, R. (1998). *Professional Learning Communities at Work: Best practices for enhancing student achievement.* Bloomington, IN: Solution Tree Press.

DuFour, R., & Mattos, M. (2013). How do principals really improve schools? *Educational Leadership, 70*(7), 34–40.

Durlak, J. A., & DuPre, E. P. (2008). Implementation matters: A review of research on the influence of implementation on program outcomes and the factors affecting implementation. *American Journal of Community Psychology, 41*(3–4), 327–350.

Eaker, R., & Dillard, H. (2017, Fall). Why collaborate? Because it enhances student learning. *AllThingsPLC Magazine,* 46–47.

Eaker, R., & Friziellie, H. (2017, Winter). Teacher collaboration matters a lot. *AllThingsPLC Magazine,* 42–44.

Eastwood, K. W., & Louis, K. S. (1992). Restructuring that lasts: Managing the performance dip. *Journal of School Leadership, 2*(2), 212–224.

Erkens, C., & Twadell, E. (2012). *Leading by design: An action framework for PLC at Work leaders.* Bloomington, IN: Solution Tree Press.

Forbes Coaches Council. (2016). *13 Ways leaders can build a coaching culture at work.* Accessed at www.forbes.com/sites/forbescoachescouncil/2016/10/07/13-ways -leaders-can-build-a-coaching-culture-at-work/#65b9d13544b6 on December 19, 2017.

Fullan, M. (1993). *Change forces: Probing the depths of educational reform.* Levittown, PA: Falmer Press.

Fullan, M. (2005). *Leadership and sustainability: System thinkers in action.* Thousand Oaks, CA: Corwin Press.

Fulton, K., & Britton, T. (2011). *STEM teachers in professional learning communities: From good teachers to great teaching.* Washington, DC: National Commission on Teaching and America's Future.

Fulton, K., Yoon, I., & Lee, C. (2005). *Induction into learning communities.* Washington, DC: National Commission on Teaching and America's Future.

Garmston, R., Linder, C., & Whitaker, J. (1993). Reflections on cognitive coaching. *Educational Leadership, 51*(2), 57–61.

Garmston, R. J. (1987). How administrators support peer coaching. *Educational Leadership, 44*(5), 18–26.

Garmston, R. J., & Wellman, B. M. (2016). *The adaptive school: A sourcebook for developing collaborative groups* (3rd ed.). Lanham, MD: Rowman & Littlefield.

Gates, B. (2013, May). *Teachers need real feedback* [Video file]. Accessed at www.ted .com/talks/bill_gates_teachers_need_real_feedback on July 12, 2017.

Graham, P., & Ferriter, B. (2008). One step at a time. *Journal of Staff Development, 29*(3), 38–42.

Guskey, T. R. (2007/2008). The rest of the story: The power of formative classroom assessment depends on how you use the results. *Educational Leadership, 65*(4), 28–35.

Hall, P., & Simeral, A. (2015). *Teach, reflect, learn: Building your capacity for success in the classroom.* Alexandria, VA: Association for Supervision and Curriculum Development.

Hanover Research. (2015). *Best practices in instructional coaching: Prepared for Iowa Area Education Agencies.* Arlington, VA: Author.

Harmony Education Center. (2014). *National School Reform Faculty protocols and activities . . . from A to Z.* Accessed at www.nsrfharmony.org/free-resources /protocols/a-z on March 2, 2017.

Hattie, J. (2009). *Visible learning: A synthesis of over 800 meta-analyses relating to achievement.* New York: Routledge.

Hattie, J. (2012). *Visible learning for teachers: Maximizing impact on learning.* New York: Routledge.

Hattie, J. (2015a). The applicability of visible learning to higher education. *Scholarship of Teaching and Learning in Psychology, 1*(1), 79–91.

Hattie, J. (2015b). *What doesn't work in education: The politics of distraction.* London: Pearson.

Hattie, J. (2015c). *What works best in education: The politics of collaborative expertise.* London: Pearson.

Hess, K. (n.d.). *Cognitive rigor and depth of knowledge.* Accessed at www.karin-hess .com/cognitive-rigor-and-dok on July 12, 2017.

Jolly, A. (2008). *Team to teach: A facilitator's guide to professional learning teams.* Oxford, OH: National Staff Development Council.

Joyce, B., & Showers, B. (2002). *Student achievement through staff development* (3rd ed.). Alexandria, VA: Association for Supervision and Curriculum Development.

Kang, G. Y. (2016). The value of coaching: Collaborative relationships spur professional growth. *Journal of Staff Development, 37*(5), 49–52.

Killion, J. (2015). *The feedback process: Transforming feedback for professional learning.* Oxford, OH: Learning Forward.

Killion, J., & Harrison, C. (2006). *Taking the lead: New roles for teachers and school-based coaches.* Oxford, OH: National Staff Development Council.

Killion, J., & Harrison, C. (2017). *Taking the lead: New roles for teachers and school-based coaches* (2nd ed.). Oxford, OH: Learning Forward.

Killion, J., Harrison, C., Bryan, C., & Clifton, H. (2012). *Coaching matters.* Oxford, OH: Learning Forward.

King, D., Neuman, M., Pelchat, J., Potochnik, T., Rao, S., & Thompson, J. (2004). *Instructional coaching: Professional development strategies that improve instruction.* Providence, RI: Annenberg Institute for School Reform.

Knight, D. S. (2017). *Assessing the cost of instructional coaching.* Accessed at www
.researchgate.net/publication/236780276_Assessing_the_Cost_of_Instructional
_Coaching on December 8, 2017.

Knight, G. (2014, January 6). *3 characteristics of effective feedback* [Blog post].
Accessed at www.insideoutdev.com/pivot-point/2014/01/3-characteristics-of
-effective-feedback on July 12, 2017.

Knight, J. (2004). Instructional coaching. *Stratenotes, 13*(3), 1–5.

Knight, J. (2007). *Instructional coaching: A partnership approach to improving
instruction.* Thousand Oaks, CA: Corwin Press.

Knight, J., Elford, M., Hock, M., Dunekack, D., Bradley, B., Deshler, D. D., et al.
(2015). 3 steps to great coaching: A simple but powerful instructional coaching
cycle nets results. *Journal of Staff Development, 36*(1), 10–12, 14, 16, 18.

Kraft, M. A., Blazar, D., & Hogan, D. (2017). *The effect of teacher coaching on
instruction and achievement: A meta-analysis of the causal evidence* (Working
paper). Providence, RI: Brown University.

LeaderSpace. (2014). *Team coaching: The future of leadership development; an interview
with Richard Boston managing director at LeaderSpace.* London: Author. Accessed
at www.leader-space.com/wp-content/uploads/2014/03/Team-coaching-the
-future-of-leadership-development.pdf on December 17, 2017.

Leana, C. R. (2011). The missing link in school reform. *Stanford Social Innovation
Review.* Accessed at http//ssir.org/articles/entry/the_missing _link_in_school
_reform on July 12, 2017.

Leithwood, K., & Louis, K. S. (2012). *Linking leadership to student learning.* San
Francisco: Jossey-Bass.

Lemov, D., Woolway, E., & Yezzi, K. (2012). *Perfect practice: 42 rules for getting better
at getting better.* San Francisco, CA: Jossey-Bass.

Lipton, L., & Wellman, B. M. (2001). *Mentoring matters: A practical guide to
learning-focused relationships.* Sherman, CT: MiraVia.

Liska, C. (2013). *What, exactly, is coaching? The core competencies* [Blog post]. Accessed
at www.td.org/Publications/Blogs/Human-Capital-Blog/2013/11/What-Exactly
-Is-Coaching-the-Core-Competencies on November 4, 2017.

Little, J. W. (1990a). Teachers as colleagues. In A. Lieberman (Ed.), *Schools as
collaborative cultures: Creating the future now* (pp. 165–193). Bristol, PA: Falmer
Press.

Louis, K. S., Leithwood, K., Wahlstrom, K. L., & Anderson, S. E. (2010). *Investigating the links to improved student learning: Final report of research findings.* Minneapolis, MN: Center for Applied Research and Educational Improvement.

Many, T. (2016, October). *High-leverage strategies for school leaders: A focus on learning.* Lecture presented at Macomb Intermediate School District, Clinton Township, MI.

Many, T. W., & Sparks-Many, S. K. (2015). *Leverage: Using PLCs to promote lasting improvement in schools.* Thousand Oaks, CA: Corwin Press.

Marshall, K. (2017, March 8). The Marshall memo: Instructional coaching is an ideal form of PD—except when it isn't. *The International Educator, 676.*

Marzano, R. J. (2003). *What works in schools: Translating research into action.* Alexandria, VA: Association for Supervision and Curriculum Development.

Marzano, R. J. (2017). *The PLC process and high reliability schools.* Presented at the Summit on PLC at Work, Phoenix, AZ.

McLaughlin, M. W., & Talbert, J. E. (2006). *Building school-based teacher learning communities: Professional strategies to improve student achievement.* New York: Teachers College Press.

Mirel, J., & Goldin, S. (2012, April 17). Alone in the classroom: Why teachers are too isolated. *The Atlantic.* Accessed at www.theatlantic.com/national/archive/2012/04 /alone-in-the-classroom-why-teachers-are-too-isolated/255976 on October 27, 2017.

Moody, M., & Stricker, J. (2015, November 13). *Calibrating coaches: 4 reasons to foster great instructional coaching* [Blog post]. Accessed at http://blogs.edweek.org /edweek/education_futures/2015/11/calibrating_coaches_4_reasons_to_create_a _vision_for_great_instructional_coaching.html on July 12, 2017.

Mourshed, M., Chijioke, C., & Barber, M. (2010). How the world's most improved school systems keep getting better. Accessed at www.teindia.nic.in/Files/Articles /How-the-Worlds-Most-Improved-School-Systems-Keep-Getting-Better _Download-version_Final.pdf on December 8, 2017.

Nagel, D. (2015). *Effective grading practices for secondary teachers: Practical strategies to prevent failure, recover credits, and increase standards-based/referenced grading.* Thousand Oaks, CA: Corwin Press.

National Commission on Teaching and America's Future. (2003). *No dream denied: A pledge to America's children.* Washington, DC: Author.

National Governors Association Center for Best Practices & Council of Chief State School Officers. (2010a). *Common Core State Standards for English language arts and literacy in history/social studies, science, and technical subjects.* Washington, DC: Authors. Accessed at www.corestandards.org/assets/CCSSI_ELA%20Standards .pdf on August 21, 2017.

National Governors Association Center for Best Practices & Council of Chief State School Officers. (2010b). *Common Core State Standards for mathematics.* Washington, DC: Authors. Accessed at www.corestandards.org/assets/CCSSI _Math%20Standards.pdf on September 11, 2017.

Neufeld, B., & Roper, D. (2003). *Coaching: A strategy for developing instructional capacity—Promises and practicalities.* Washington, DC: Aspen Institute Program on Education. Accessed at www.annenberginstitute.org/sites/default/files /product/268/files/Coaching.pdf on July 12, 2017.

Perkins, S. J. (1998). On becoming a peer coach: Practices, identities, and beliefs of inexperienced coaches. *Journal of Curriculum and Supervision, 13*(3), 235–254.

Peterson, K. D. (2002a). Enhancing school culture: Reculturing schools. *Journal of Staff Development, 23*(3).

Peterson, K. D. (2002b). Positive or negative. *Journal of Staff Development, 23*(3), 10–15.

process. (n.d.). In *Dictionary.com.* Accessed at www.dictionary.com/browse/process?s=t on July 12, 2017.

Public Education & Business Coalition (PEBC). (2012). *PEBC Continuum of Growth in Best Instructional Practices.* Accessed at https://docs.google.com /viewer?a=v&pid=sites&srcid=ZGVmYXVsdGRvbWFpbnxzY2hzY29hY2hpbmd 8Z3g6Njg2ZmE1OWY3YWE4OTA3Mg on December 19, 2017.

Reeves, D. (2015). *Inspiring creativity and innovation in K–12.* Bloomington, IN: Solution Tree Press.

Reeves, D. B. (2004). *Accountability in action: A blueprint for learning organizations* (2nd ed.). Englewood, CO: Advanced Learning Press.

Sagie, A. (1997). Tightening the loose-tight model of leadership. *Applied Psychology, 46,* 447–452.

Schmoker, M. (2004). Learning communities at the crossroads: Toward the best schools we've ever had. *Phi Delta Kappan, 86*(1), 84–88.

Sharratt, L., & Fullan, M. (2012). *Putting FACES on the data: What great leaders do!* Thousand Oaks, CA: Corwin Press.

Shipper, F. (2009). Investigating the sustainability of a sustained 360 process. *Academy of Management Journal*, 1–6.

Showers, B. (1985). Teachers coaching teachers. *Educational Leadership*, *42*(7), 43–48.

Showers, B., & Joyce, B. (1996). The evolution of peer coaching. *Educational Leadership*, *53*(6), 12–16.

Showers, B., Joyce, B., & Bennett, B. (1987). Synthesis of research on staff development: A framework for future study and a state-of-the-art analysis. *Educational Leadership*, *45*(3), 77–87.

Showers, B., Murphy, C., & Joyce, B. (1996). The River City program: Staff development becomes school improvement. In B. Joyce & E. Calhoun (Eds.), *Learning experiences in school renewal: An exploration of five successful programs* (pp. 13–51). Eugene, OR: ERIC Clearinghouse on Educational Management.

Sparks, D. (2007). *Leading for results: Transforming teaching, learning, and relationships in schools* (2nd ed.). Thousand Oaks, CA: Corwin Press.

Sparks, S. K., & Many, T. W. (2015). *How to cultivate collaboration in a PLC*. Bloomington, IN: Solution Tree Press.

Stein, M. K., & D'Amico, L. (2002). The district as a professional learning laboratory. In A. M. Hightower, M. S. Knapp, J. A. Marsh, & M. W. McLaughlin (Eds.), *School districts and instructional renewal* (pp. 61–75). New York: Teachers College Press.

Stone, D., & Heen, S. (2014). *Thanks for the feedback: The science and art of receiving feedback well (even when it is off base, unfair, poorly delivered, and frankly, you're not in the mood)*. New York: Viking Press.

Sweeney, D. (2011). *Student-centered coaching: A guide for K–8 coaches and principals*. Thousand Oaks, CA: Corwin Press.

Sweeney, D. (2013). *Student-centered coaching at the secondary level*. Thousand Oaks, CA: Corwin Press.

Thomas, T. (2015, November 23). *Pathways for coaching collaborative teams*. Presented at East Detroit Public Schools, Eastpointe, MI.

Tomlinson, C. A. (2001). *How to differentiate instruction in mixed-ability classrooms* (2nd ed.). Alexandria, VA: Association for Supervision and Curriculum Development.

Trach, S. A. (2014). Inspired instructional coaching: Stimulate teaching by structuring meaningful observations and feedback that will improve instruction schoolwide. *Principal*, 13–16. Accessed at www.naesp.org/sites/default/files/Trach_ND14.pdf on July 12, 2017.

Trach, S. A. (2015). Instructional coaching: Leverage assistant principals. *Communicator, 39*(1). Accessed at www.naesp.org/communicator-september-2015 /instructional-coaching-leverage-assistant-principals on July 12, 2017.

Twadell, E. (2015, August 17–19). *Beyond the test: Formative assessment practices that work (and those that don't) in a PLC.* Presented at the Assessment NOW conference, Grand Rapids, MI.

Victorian Curriculum and Assessment Authority. (2014). *Characteristics of effective feedback.* Accessed at www.insight.vic.edu.au/feedback-and-reporting/characteristics -of-effective-feedback on July 12, 2017.

Walpole, S., & Blamey, K. L. (2008). Elementary literacy coaches: The reality of dual roles. *The Reading Teacher, 62*(3), 222–231.

Wellman, B. (2009). *Learning-focused supervision: Navigating difficult conversations.* Guilford, VT: MiraVia. Accessed at www/nesacenter.org/uploaded/conferences /FLC/2009/spkr_handouts/WellmanSupervision.pdf on November 9, 2017.

Wells, C., & Feun, L. (2008). What has changed? A study of three years of professional learning community work. *Planning and Changing, 39*(1), 42–66.

Wentworth, D., & Lombardi, M. (2014). *5 trends for the future of learning and development.* Accessed at https://trainingmag.com/5-trends-future-learning-and -development on November 9, 2017.

West, B., Williams, R., Manzeske, D., Liu, F., & Stonehill, R. (2016). *Jefferson County strategic compensation study comprehensive evaluation findings.* Washington, D.C.: American Institutes for Research. Accessed at www.jeffcopublicschools .org/community_portal/research_surveys/r_a_d_publications_and_presentations on November 9, 2017.

West Virginia Department of Education. (2006–2007). *Collegial coaching toolkit.* Charleston, WV: Author.

WestEd. (2000). *Teachers who learn, kids who achieve: A look at schools with model professional development.* San Francisco: Author.

Western Regional Educational Laboratory. (2002). *Teachers who learn, kids who achieve: A look at schools with model teacher development.* San Francisco: Author.

Wiggins, G. (2010, May 22). *Feedback: How learning occurs* [Blog post]. Accessed at www.authenticeducation.org/ae_bigideas/article.lasso?artId=61 on July 12, 2017.

Wiggins, G. (2012). Seven keys to effective feedback. *Educational Leadership, 70*(1), 10–16.

Wiliam, D. (2007). Content *then* process: Teacher learning communities in the service of formative assessment. In D. Reeves (Ed.), *Ahead of the curve: The power of assessment to transform teaching and learning* (pp. 183–204). Bloomington, IN: Solution Tree Press.

Wiliam, D. (2011). *Embedded formative assessment.* Bloomington, IN: Solution Tree Press.

Wiliam, D. (2014). *The formative evaluation of teaching performance* (Occasional Paper No. 137). East Melbourne, Victoria, Australia: Centre for Strategic Education.

Williams, K. E. (2011). *What is the future of coaching?* Accessed at https://ezinearticles .com/?What-Is-the-Future-of-Coaching?&id=6712868 on November 4, 2017.

Williams, V., & Wright, J. O. (2007). The future of executive coaching and leadership with commentary. *The International Journal of Coaching in Organizations, 5*(1), 58–76.

Wren, S. (2005, November 30–December 3). *Literacy coaches: Promises and problems.* Paper presented at the annual meeting of the National Reading Conference, Miami, FL.

Wren, S., & Vallejo, D. (2009). *Effective collaboration between instructional coaches and principals.* Accessed at www.balancedreading.com/Wren_&_Vallejo_Coach _Principal_Relatinships.pdf on July 12, 2017.

INDEX

Learning by Doing, 3rd Edition
Richard DuFour, Rebecca DuFour, Robert Eaker, Thomas W. Many, and Mike Mattos
Discover how to transform your school or district into a high-performing PLC. The third edition of this comprehensive action guide offers new strategies for addressing critical PLC topics, including hiring and retaining new staff, creating team-developed common formative assessments, and more.
BKF746

Concise Answers to Frequently Asked Questions About Professional Learning Communities at Work®
Mike Mattos, Richard DuFour, Rebecca DuFour, Robert Eaker, and Thomas W. Many
Get all of your PLC questions answered. Designed as a companion resource to Learning by Doing: A Handbook for Professional Learning Communities at Work (3rd ed.), this powerful, quick-reference guidebook is a must-have for teachers and administrators working to create and sustain the PLC process.
BKF705

How to Cultivate Collaboration in a PLC
Susan K. Sparks and Thomas W. Many
Establishing a collaborative culture can significantly impact student achievement and professional practice. With this how-to guide, you'll gain clarity on the work of teams in a PLC, uncover the elements of effective team development, and learn to navigate challenges along the way.
BKF678

AllThingsPLC Magazine
AllThingsPLC Magazine features engaging, personal commentaries from educators who have implemented the PLC process to great success. Each issue of this practical and stimulating quarterly magazine includes in-depth articles on PLC implementation and advice, websites, books, and other essential PLC resources.
CPF001

Solution Tree | Press
a division of
Solution Tree

Visit SolutionTree.com or call 800.733.6786 to order.

"Tremendous, tremendous, tremendous!

The speaker made me do some very deep internal reflection about the **PLC process** and the personal responsibility I have in making the school improvement process work **for ALL kids.**"

—Marc Rodriguez, teacher effectiveness coach, Denver Public Schools, Colorado

PD Services

Our experts draw from decades of research and their own experiences to bring you practical strategies for building and sustaining a high-performing PLC. You can choose from a range of customizable services, from a one-day overview to a multiyear process.

Book your PLC PD today!
888.763.9045

Solution Tree